Preschool Activities Book

Exciting and varied activities await your child on every page.

Activity book for 3-5 years to Learn the Alphabet, counting, complete mazes, coloring Animals, Shapes, Colors, Numbers and Letters

ISBN:978-1-916554-09-2

Yellow in nature

Green in nature

How Many?

Count the objects and write the numbers in the box

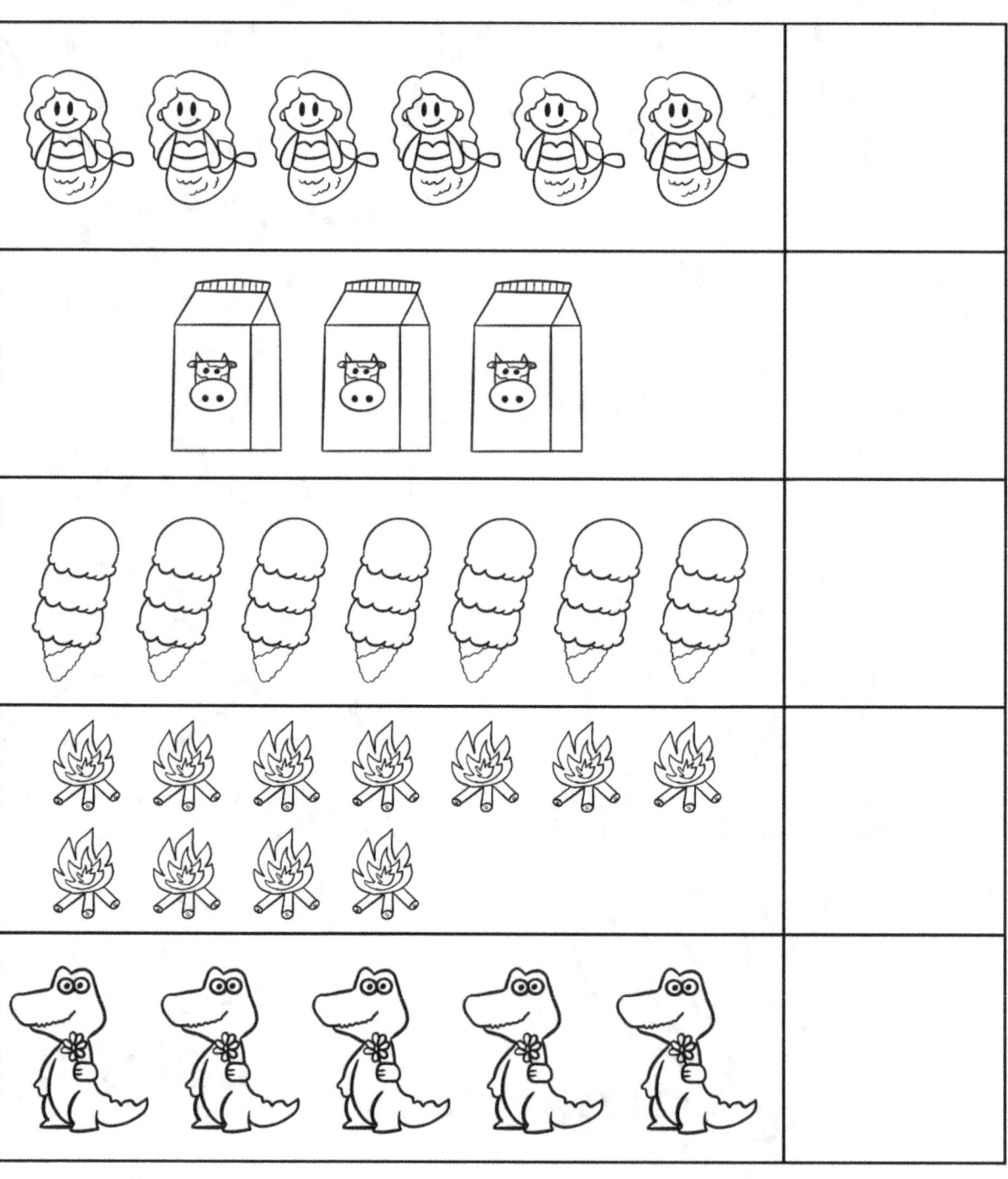

Number Matching

Match the digit with the word

12	one
6	eight
10	six
9	seven
1	ten
14	eighteen
18	two
2	twelve
7	fourteen
8	nine

Orange in nature

orange

carrot

pumpkin

PENTAGON

A is for

Amazing Ant

B is for

Brave Butterfly

D is for

Dirty Dinosaur

H is for

Happy Hedgehog

E is for

Elegant Elephant

G is for
GIANT GIRAFFE

L is for

Lazzy Lion

K is for

Kind Kangaroo

N is for

Noisy Narhwal

M is for

MIGHTY MONKEY

P is for

Playful Panda

Q is for

Quiet Quokka

S is for

Sleepy Squirrel

R is for
RARE Rhino

V is for

Vegetarian
Vulture

X is for

X-RAY XIPHIAS

W is for

Witty Walrus

Y is for Young Yak

Z is for

Zappy Zebra

My name is _____

counting & coloring

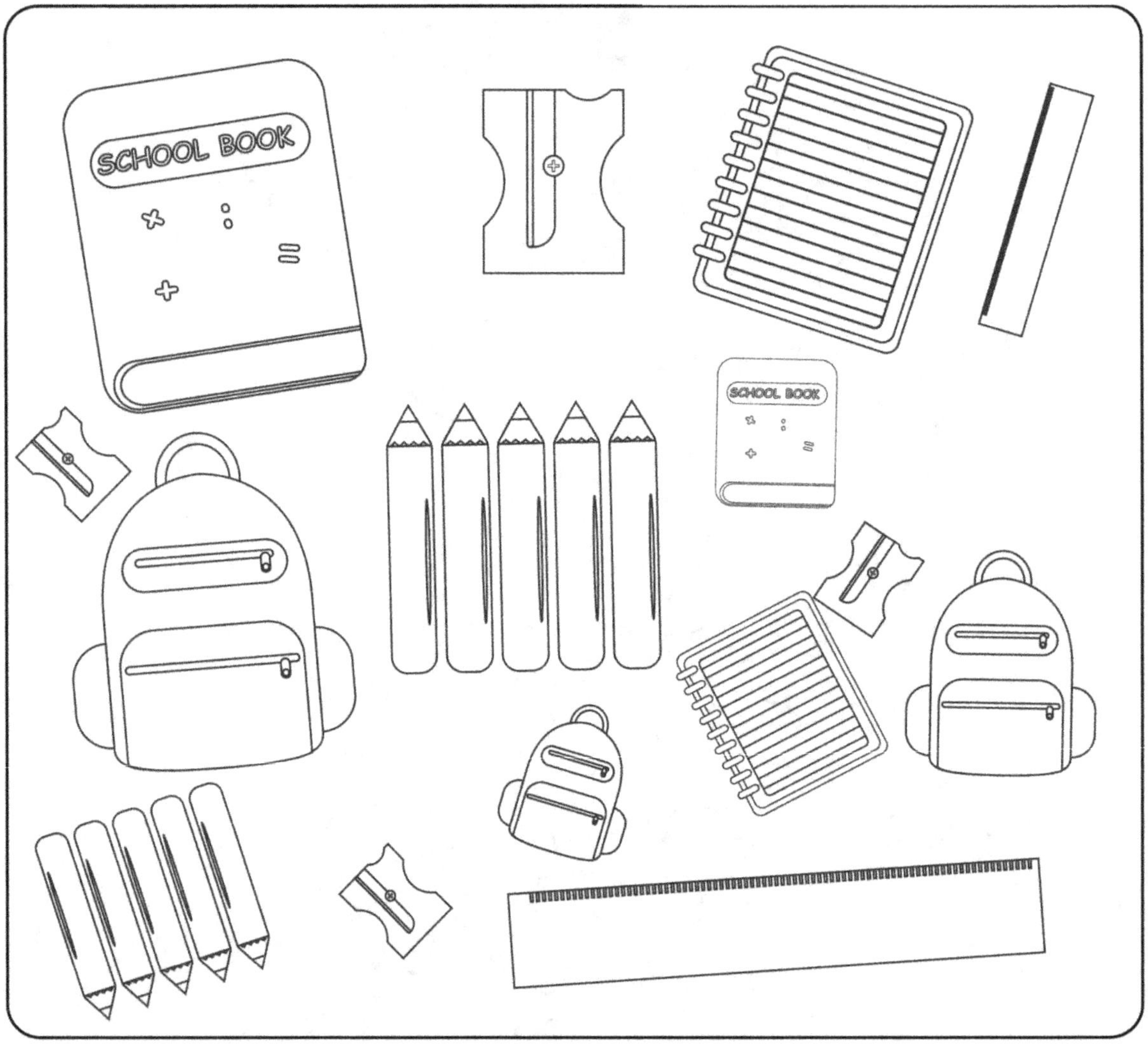

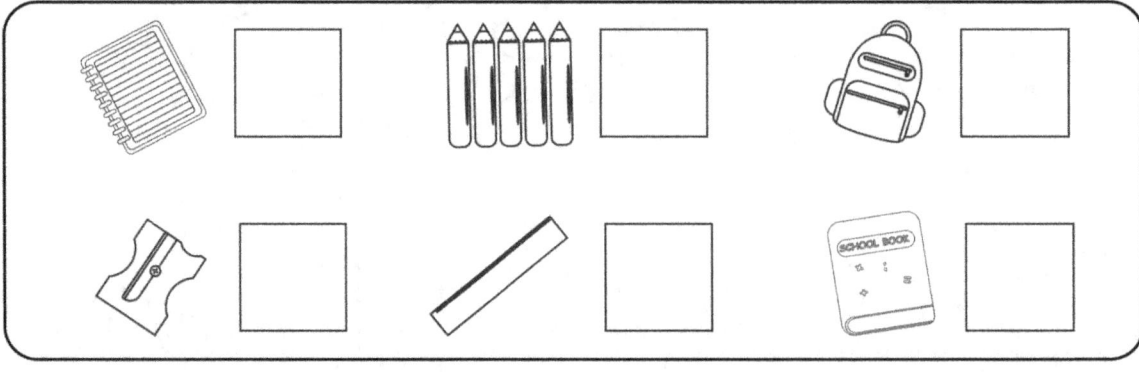

My name is _____

counting & coloring

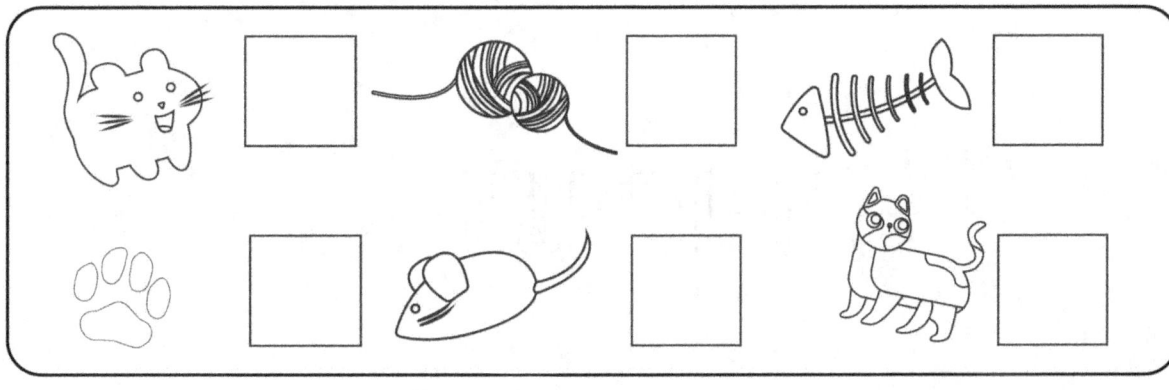

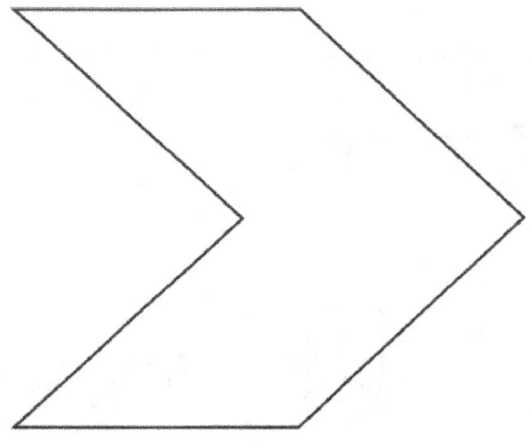

ARROW HEAD

LIGHTNING

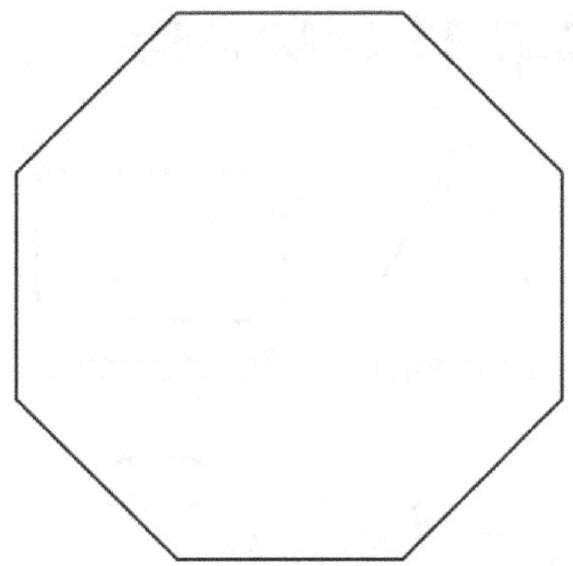

OCTAGON

HEART

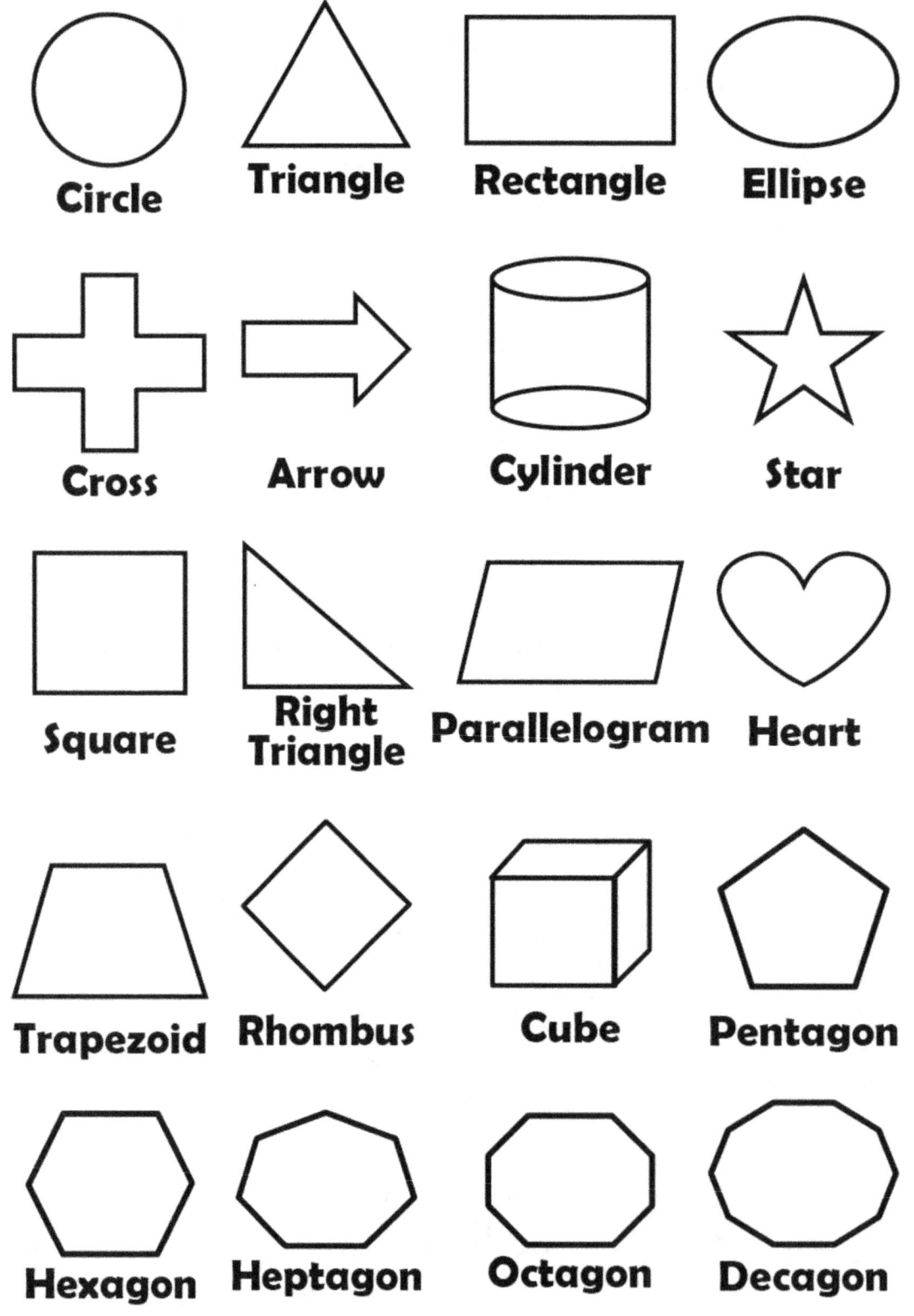

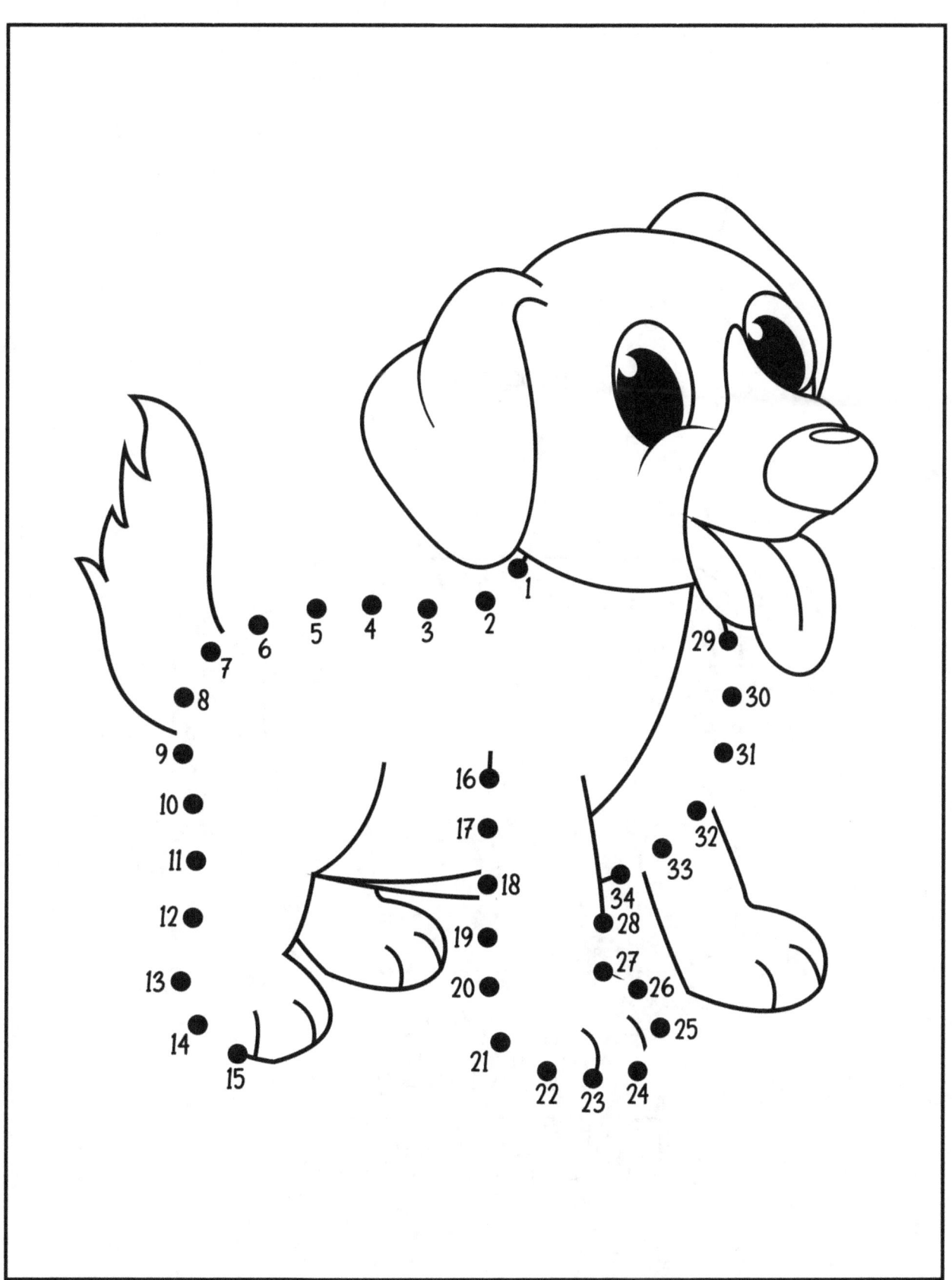

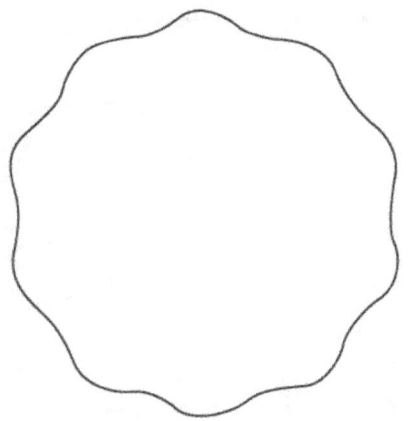

CIRCULAR
WAVE

ROUNDED
RECTANGLE

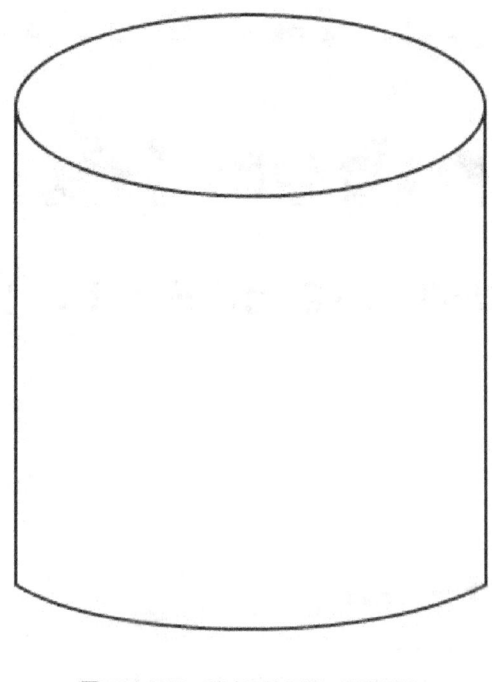

CYLINDER

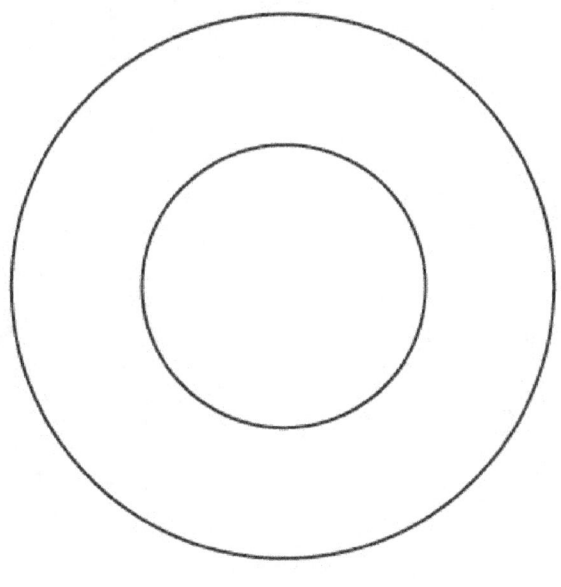

SOLID ROUND

Number Matching

Match the digit with the word

5   one

7   three

8   six

7   nine

2   ten

9   four

4   two

1   five

3   seven

10   eight

CIRCLE

RECTANGLE

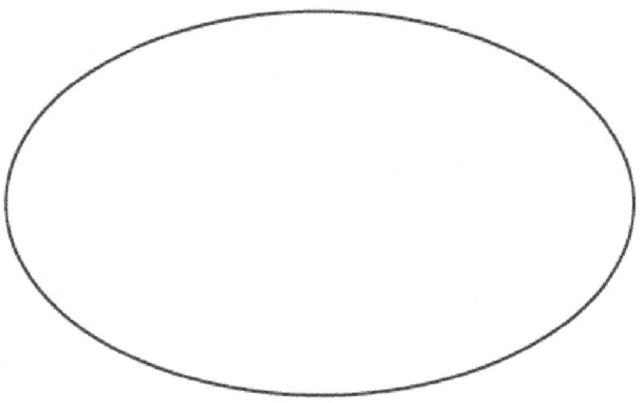

OVAL

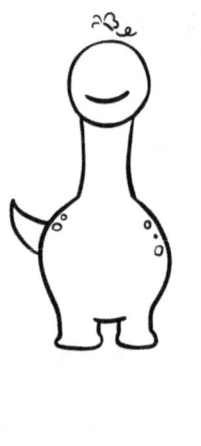
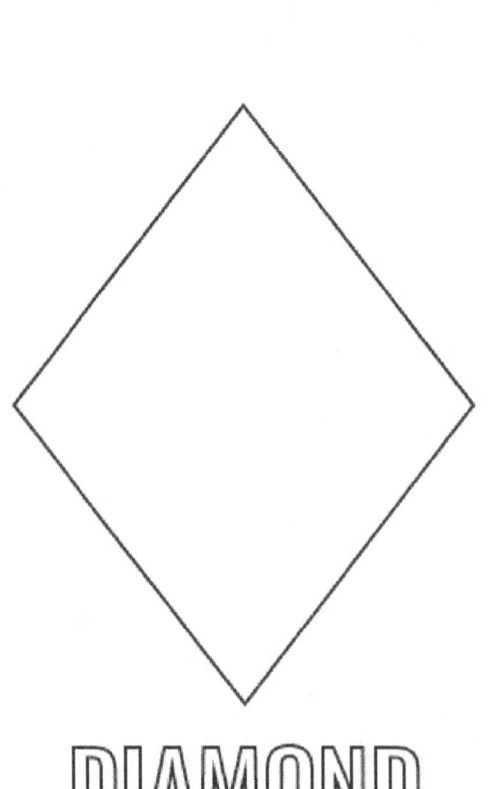

DIAMOND

How Many?

Count the objects and write the numbers in the box

Color, Count and Trace

1 1 1 1 1 1

ONE ONE ONE

one one one

Color, Count and Trace

2 2 2 2 2

TWO TWO

two two

Color, Count and Trace

Color, Count and Trace

Color, Count and Trace

Color, Count and Trace

7 7 7 7 7 7 7

SEVEN   SEVEN

seven   seven

Color, Count and Trace

Color, Count and Trace

Color, Count and Trace

Color, Count and Trace

Color, Count and Trace

Color, Count and Trace

Color, Count and Trace

Color, Count and Trace

Color, Count and Trace

Color, Count and Trace

Color, Count and Trace

Color, Count and Trace

COUNTING & COLORING

NAME: _____   DATE: _____   SCORE: _____

COUNTING & COLORING

NAME: .... DATE: .... SCORE: ......

COUNTING & COLORING

NAME: _____ DATE: _____ SCORE: _____

COUNTING & COLORING

NAME: _____ DATE: _____ SCORE: _____

COUNTING & COLORING

NAME: .... DATE: .... SCORE: ......

COUNTING & COLORING

NAME: .... DATE: .... SCORE: ......

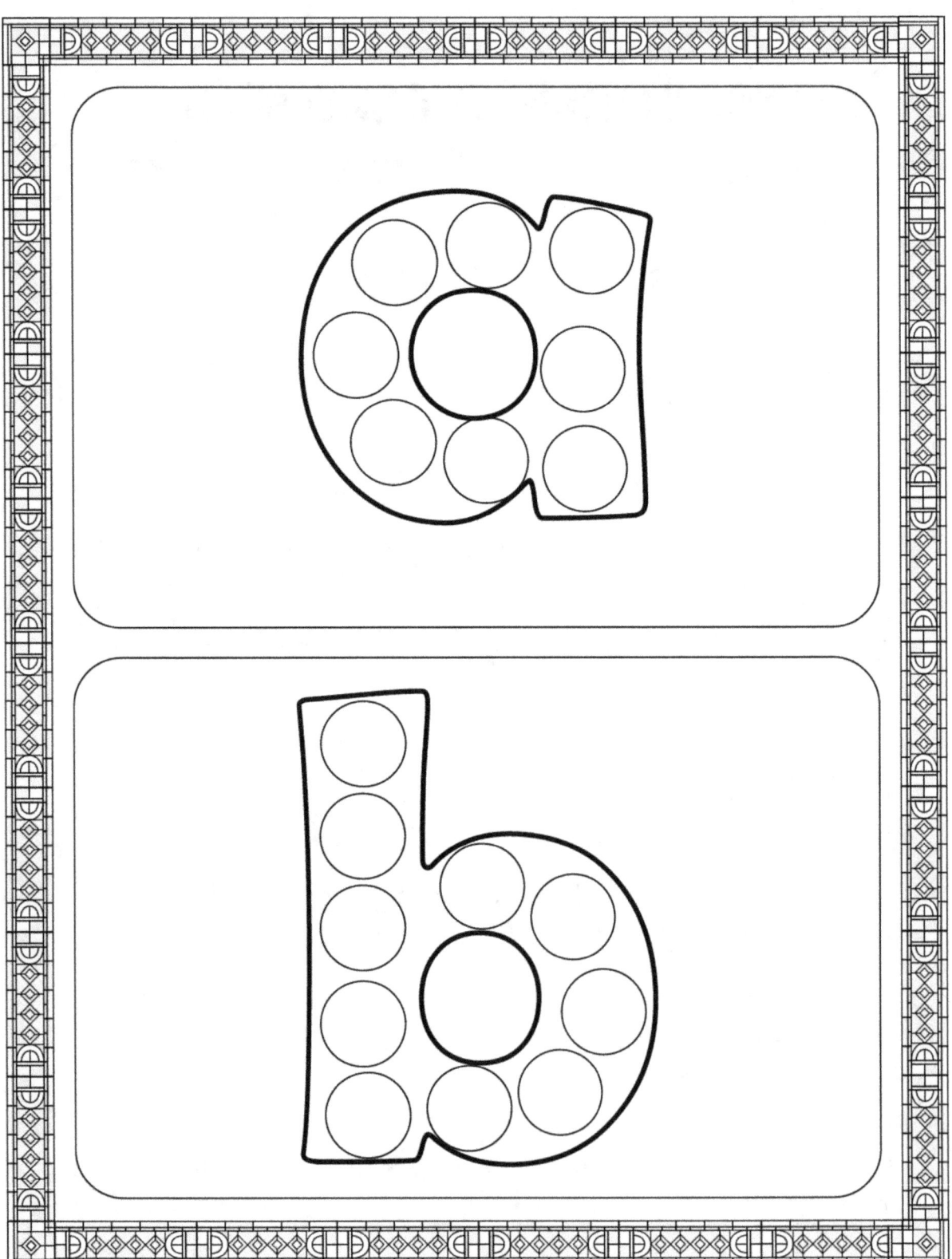

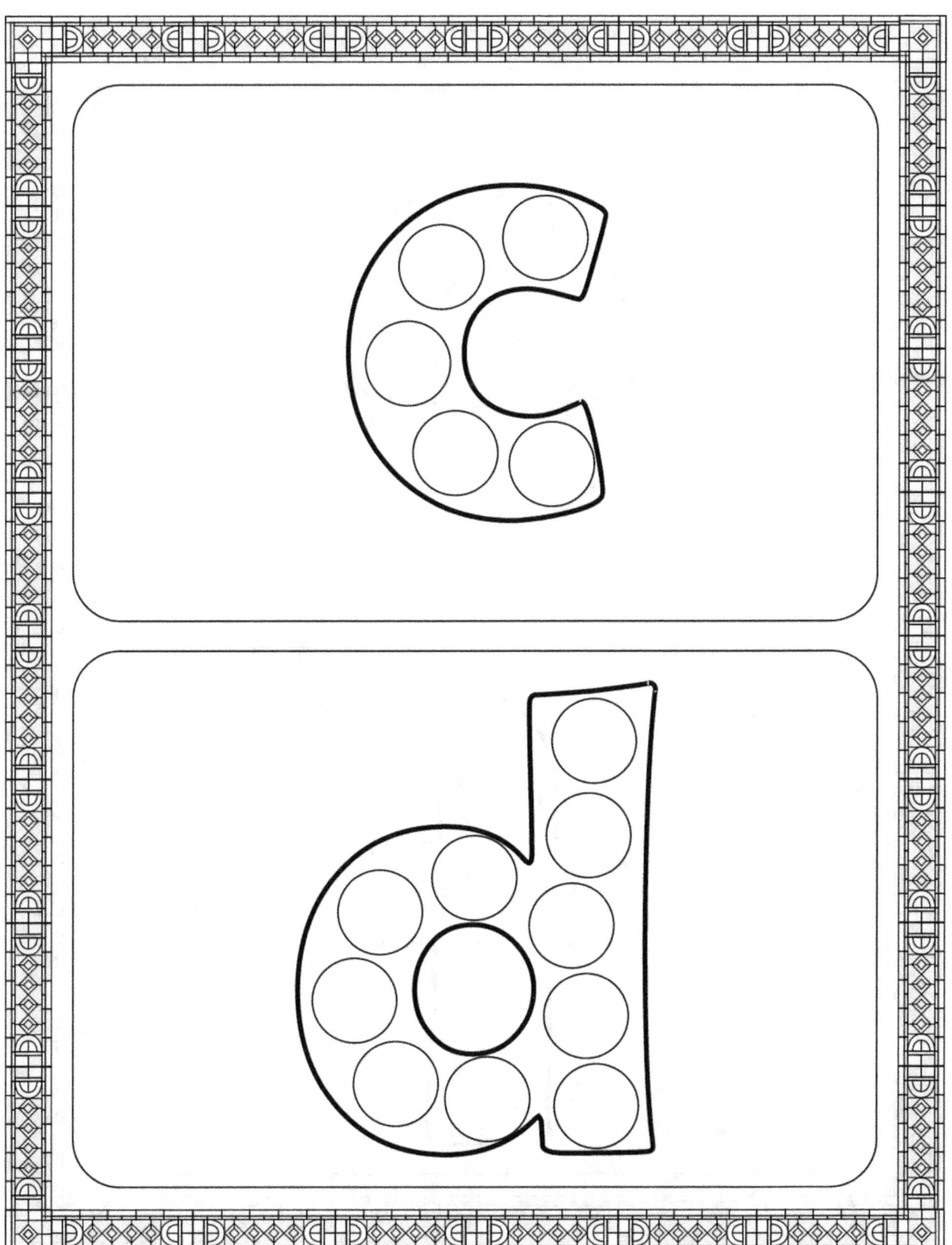

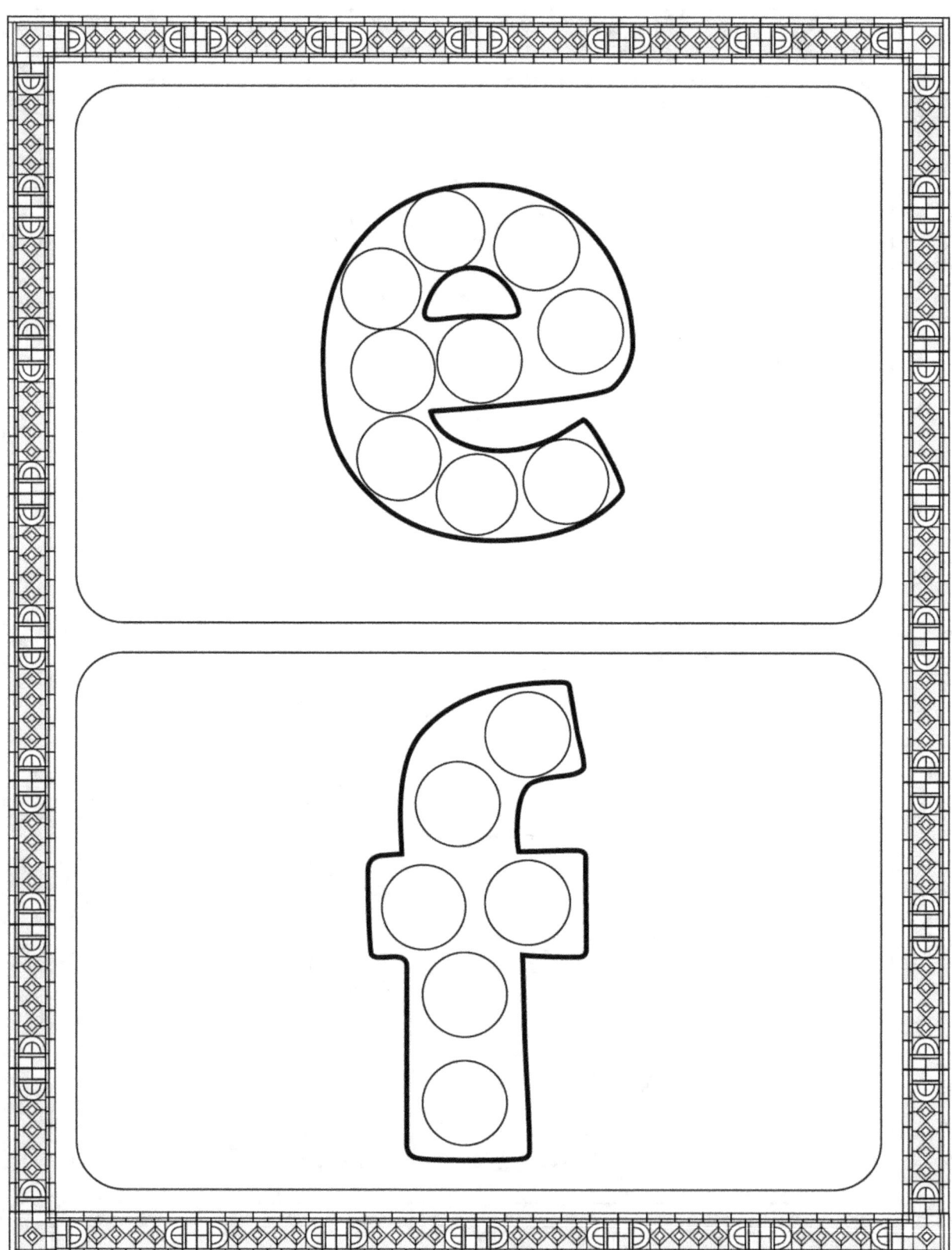

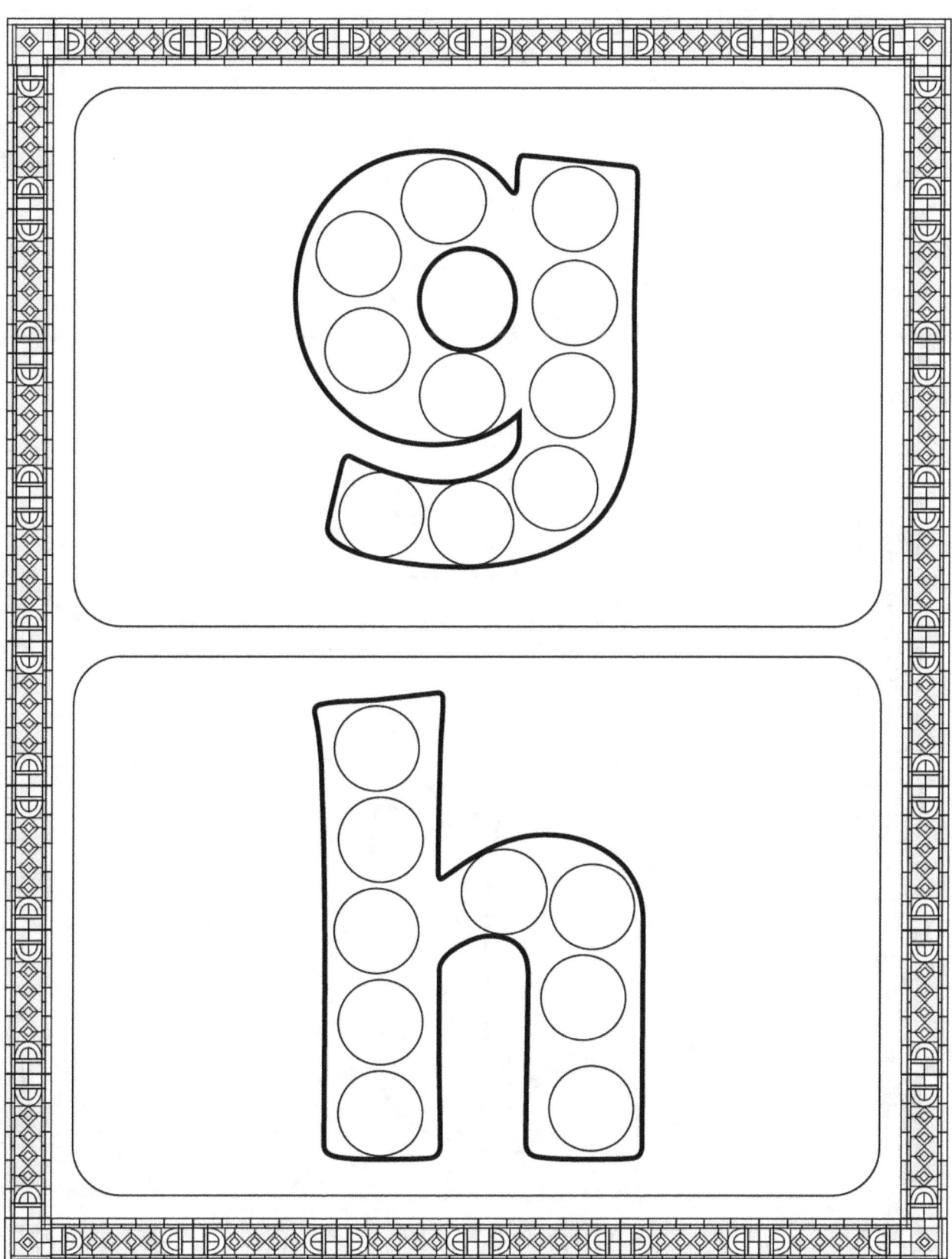

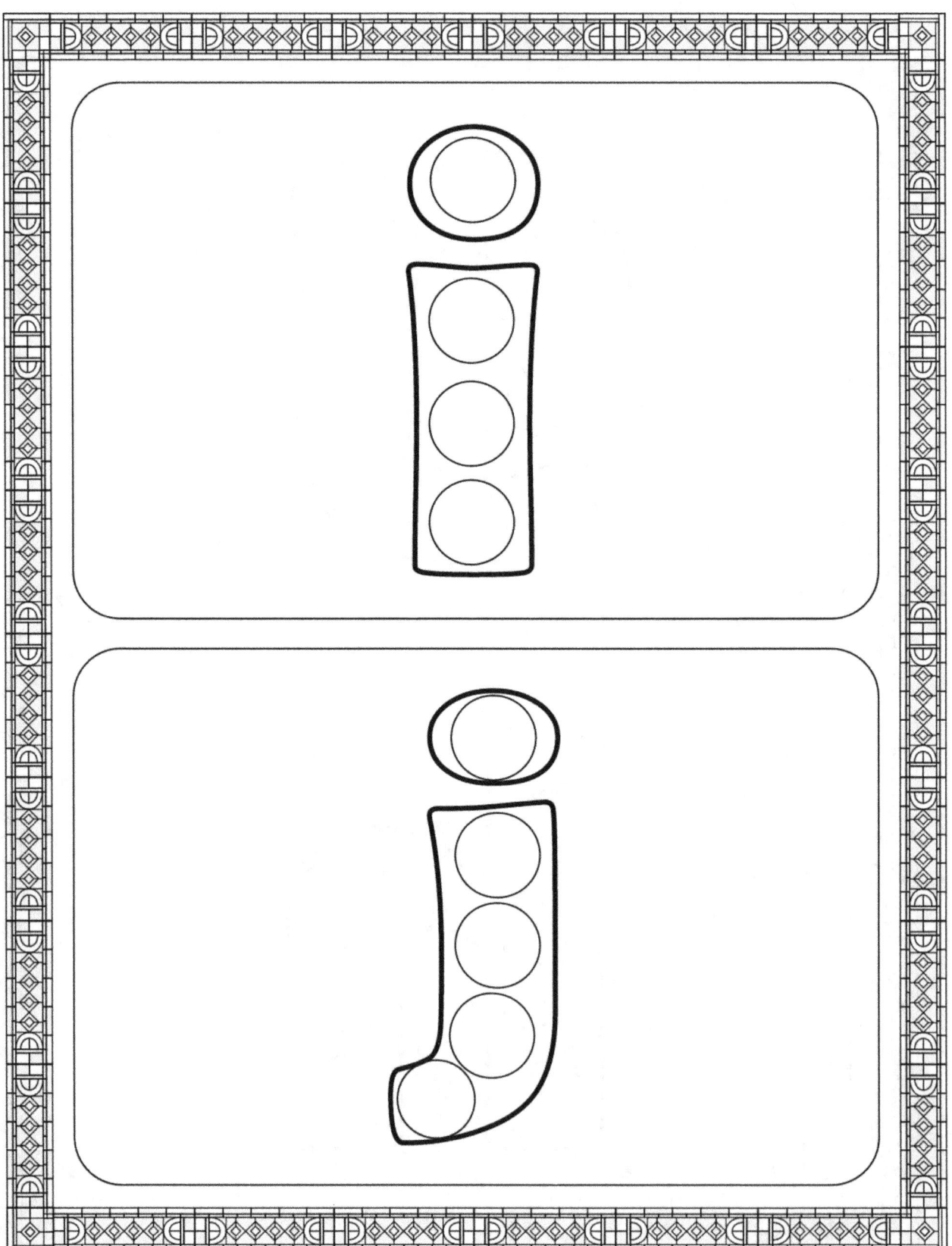

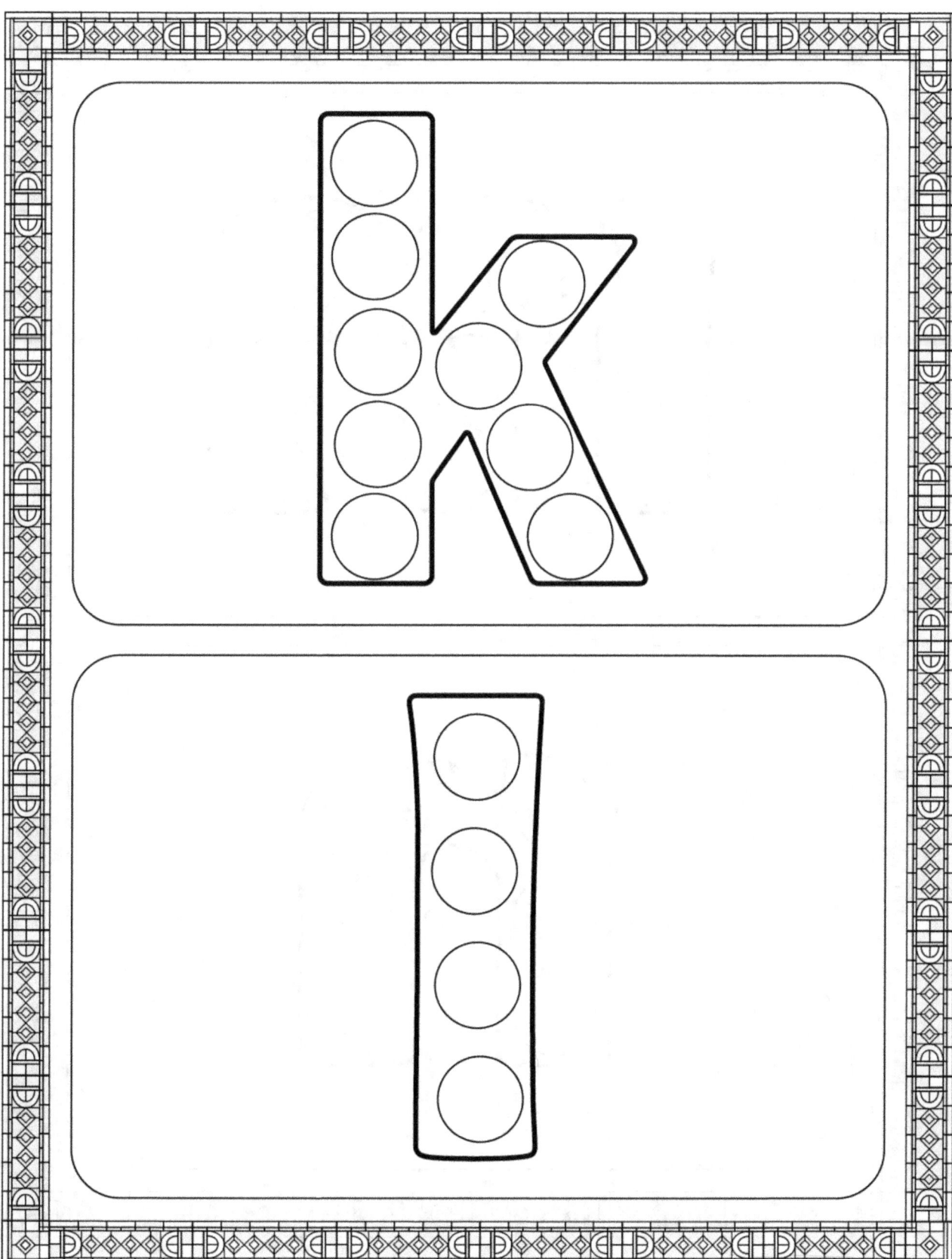

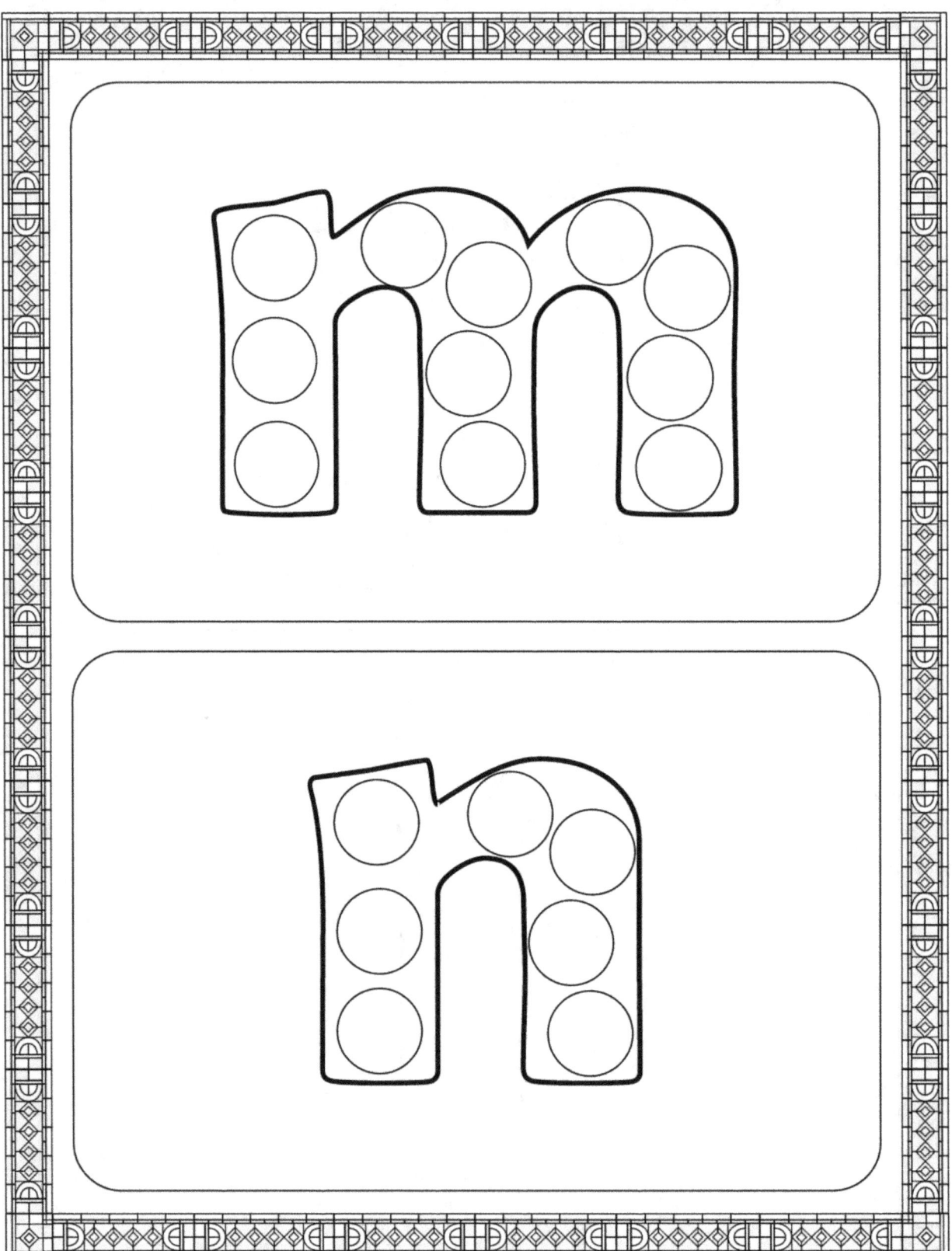

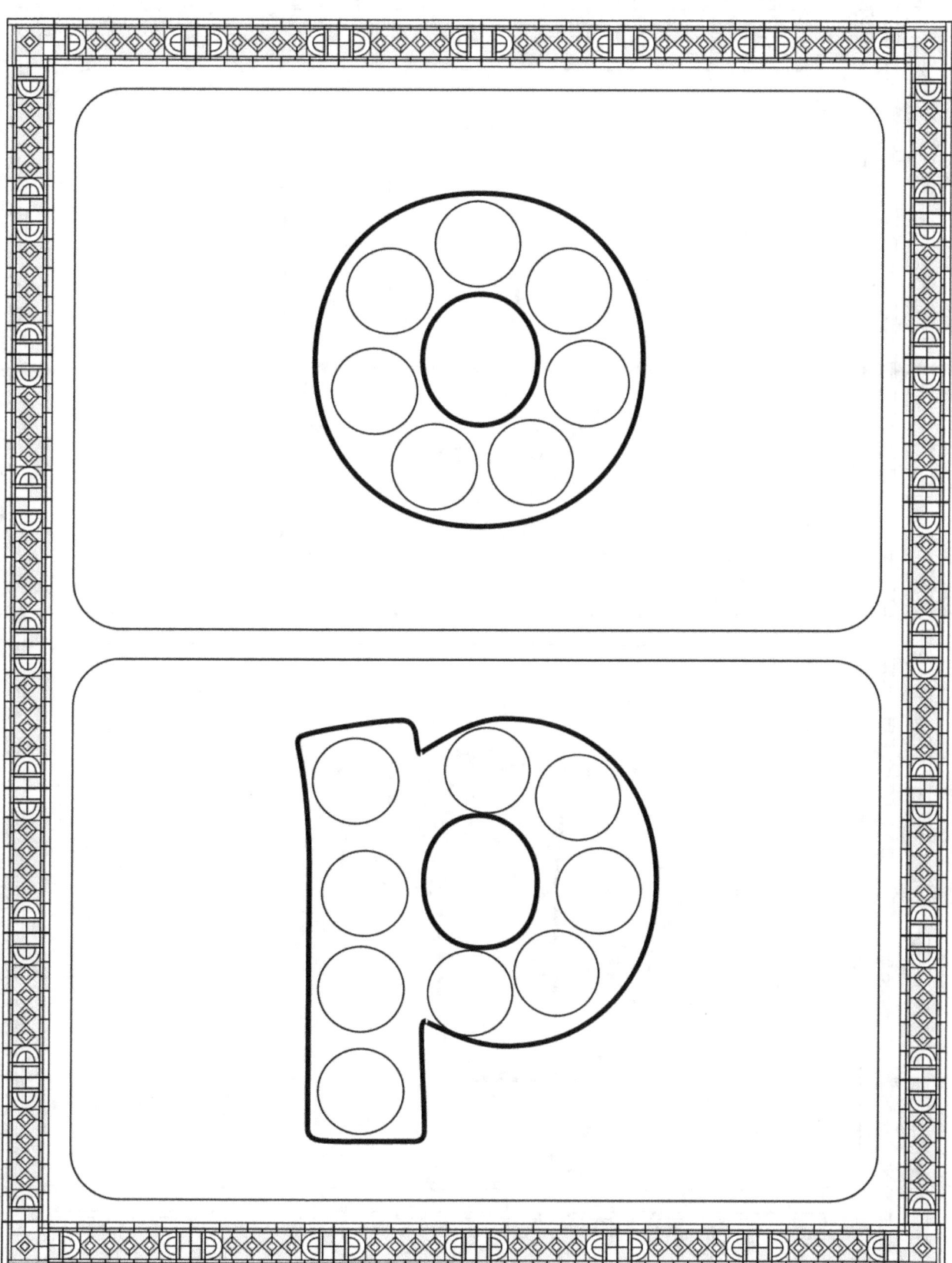

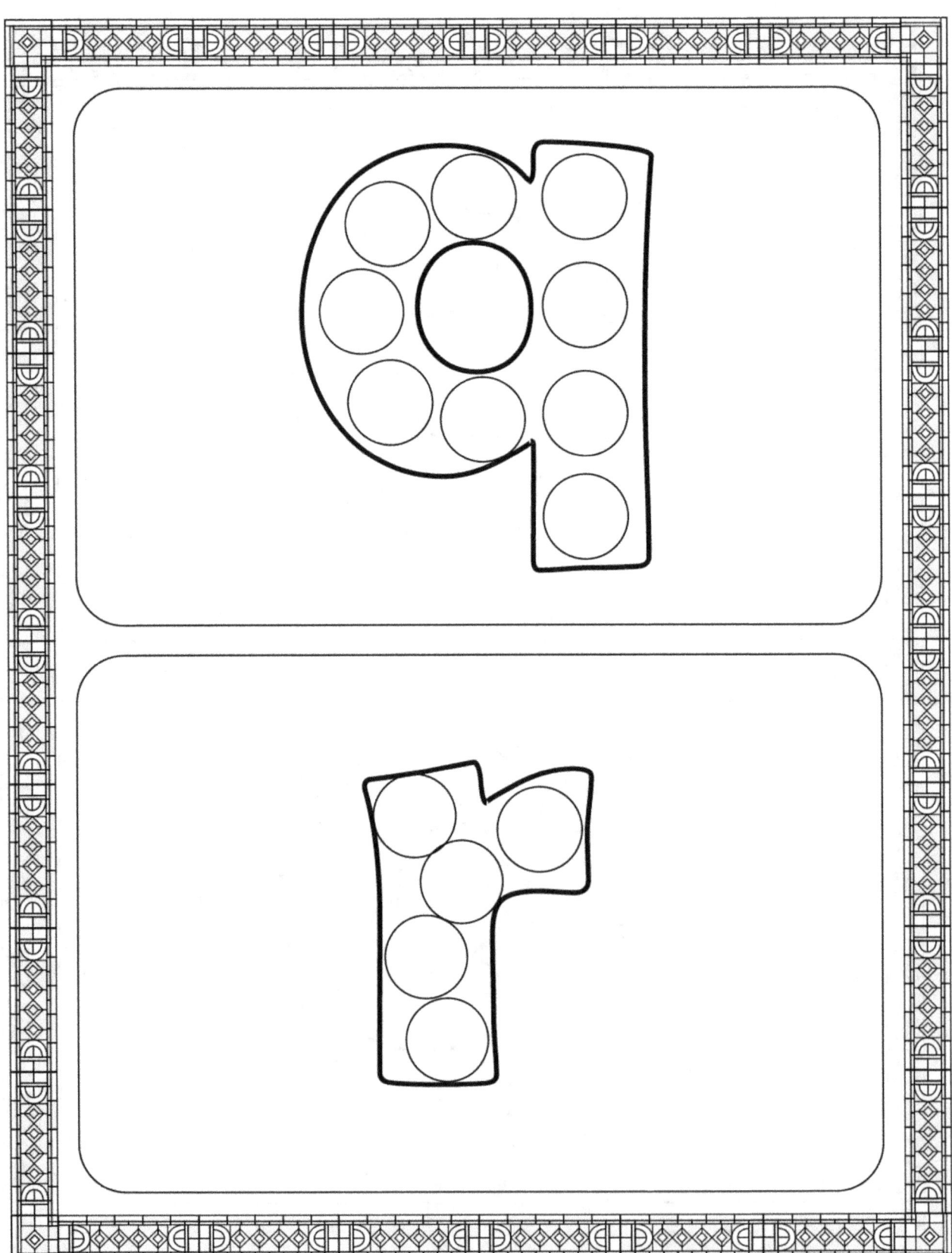

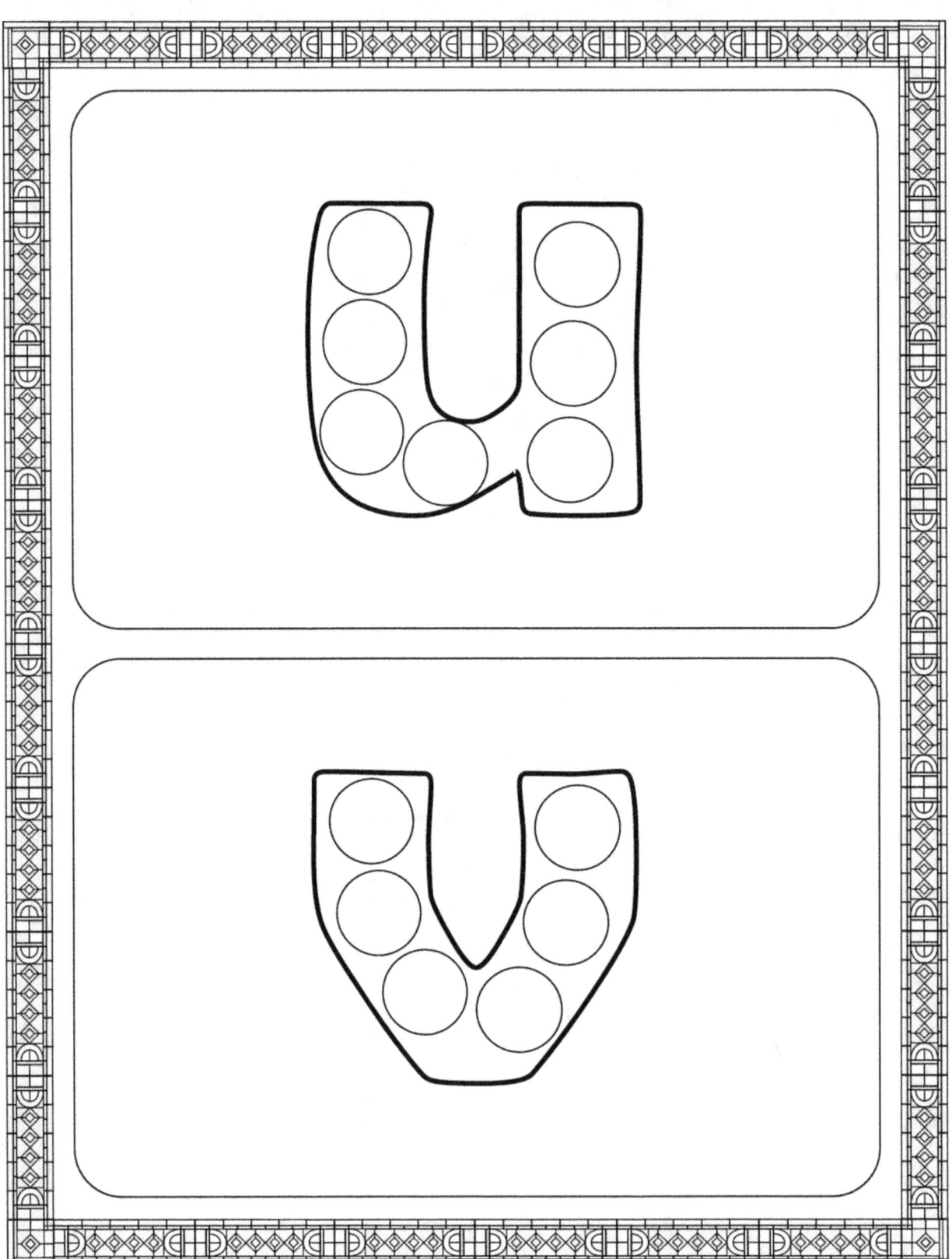

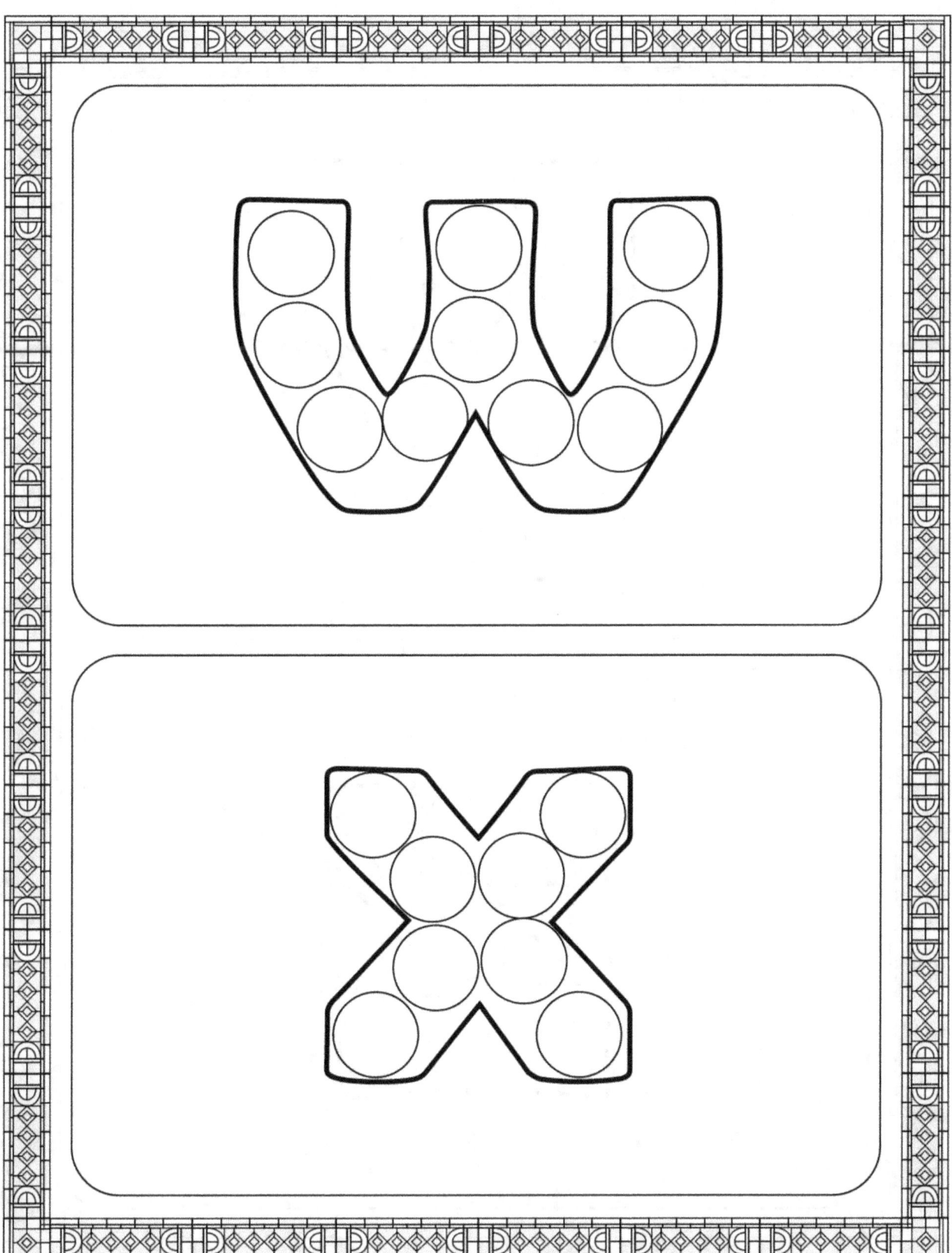

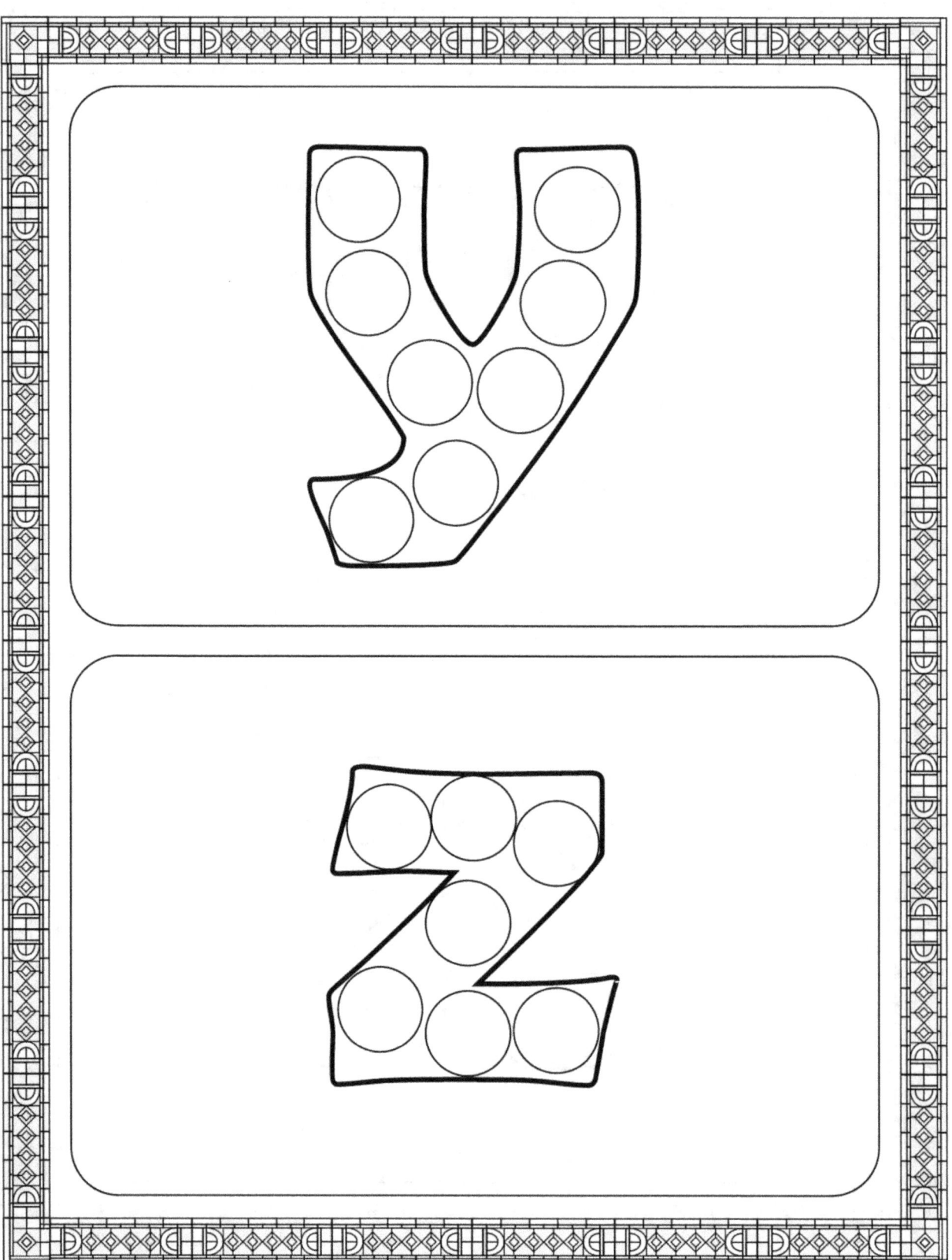

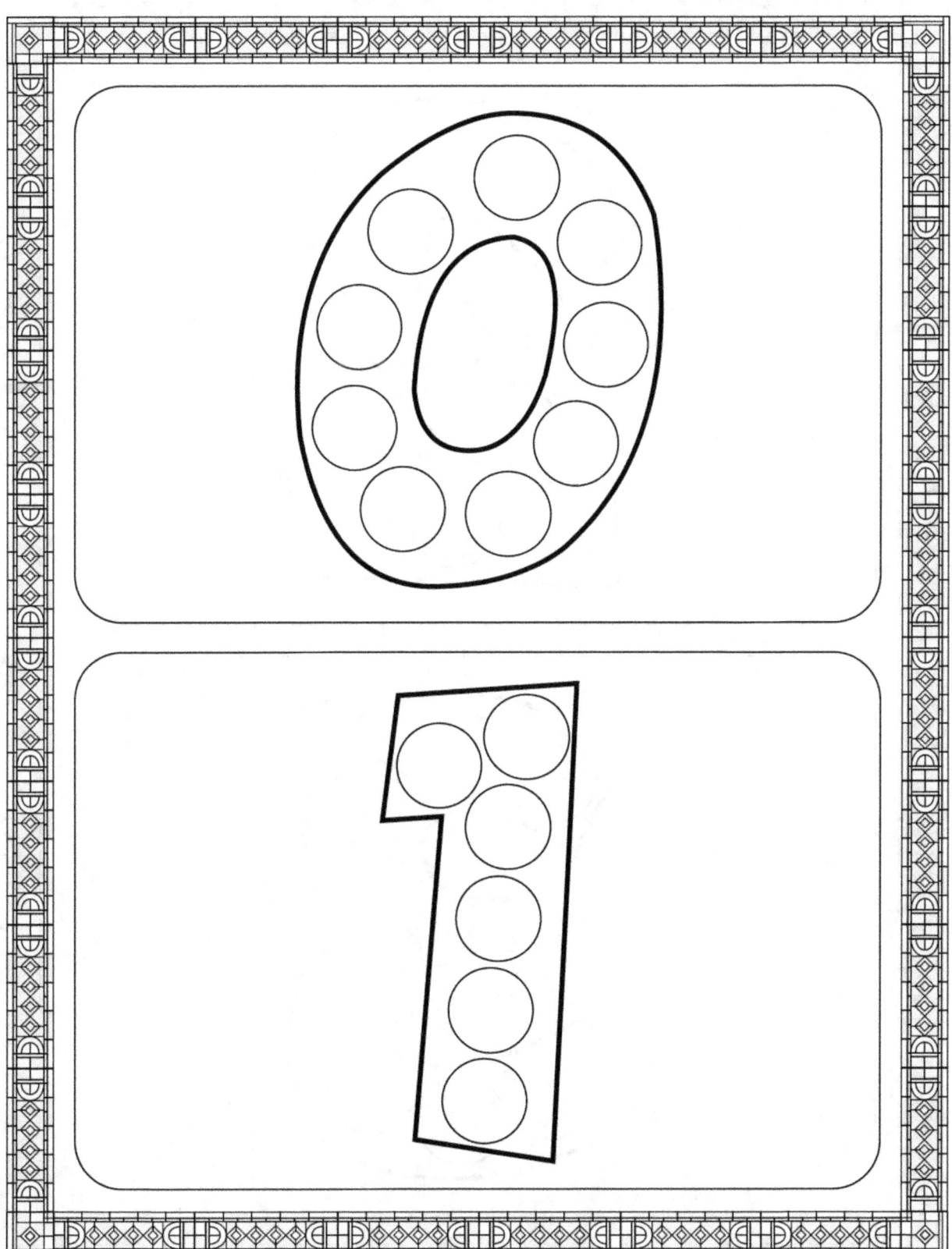

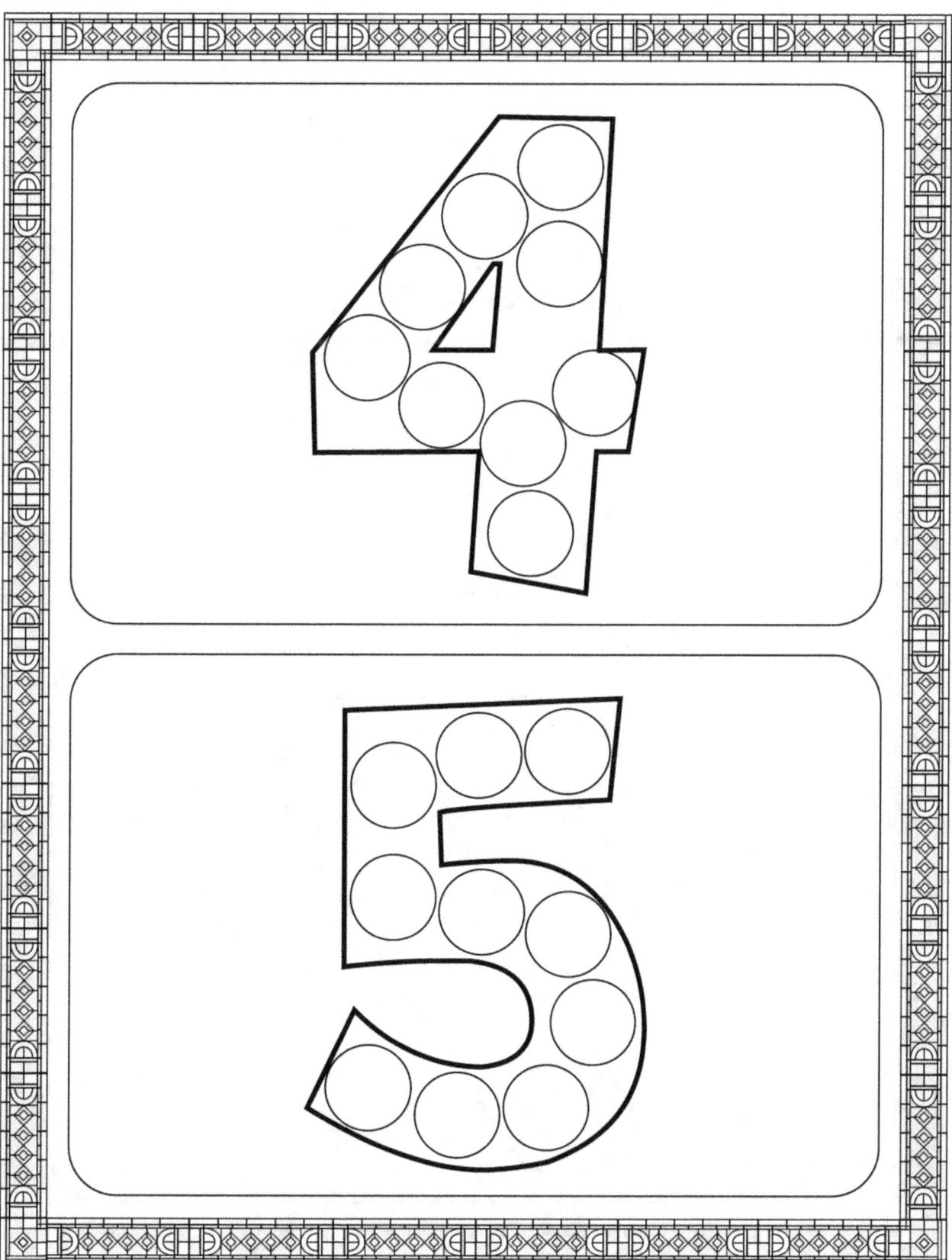

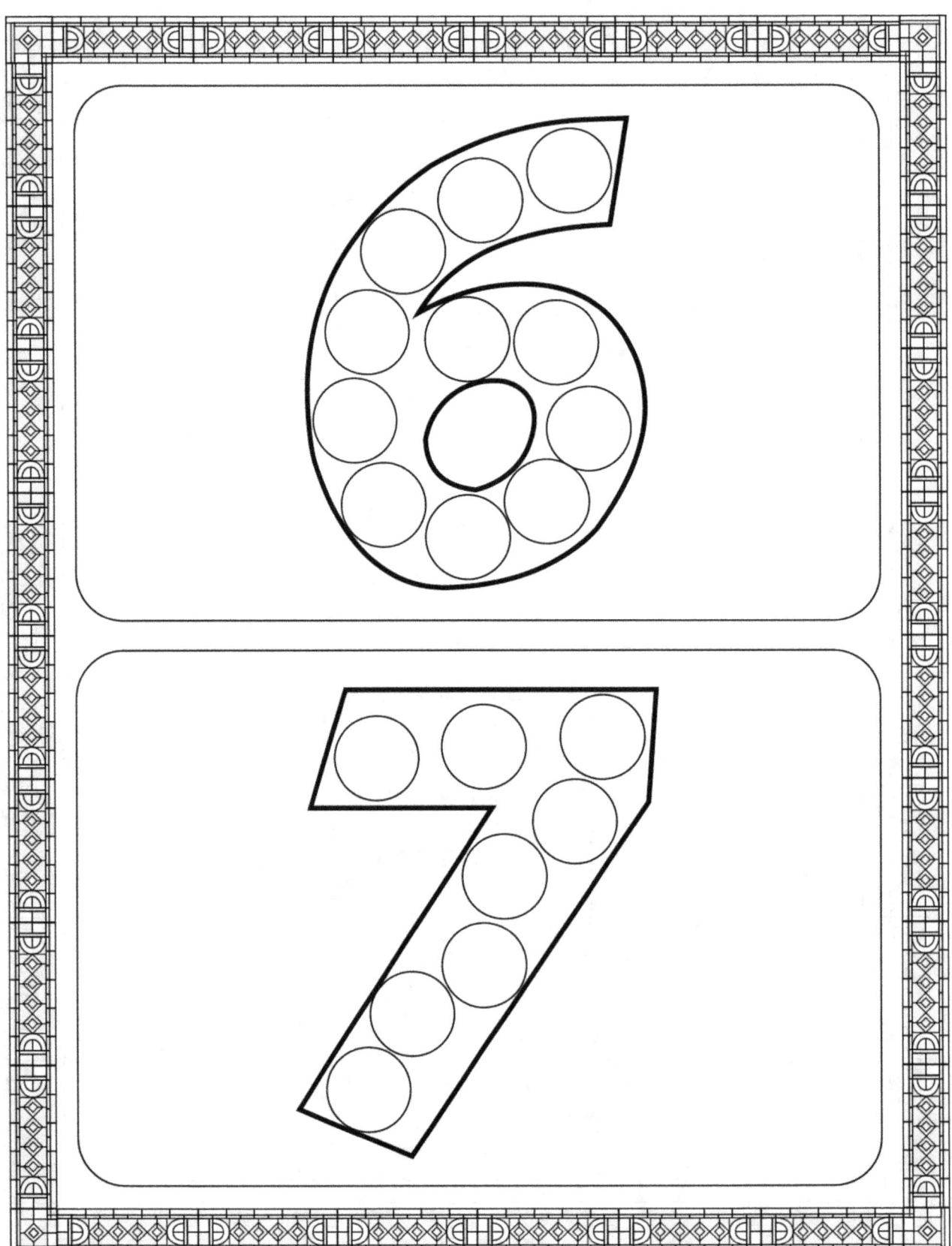

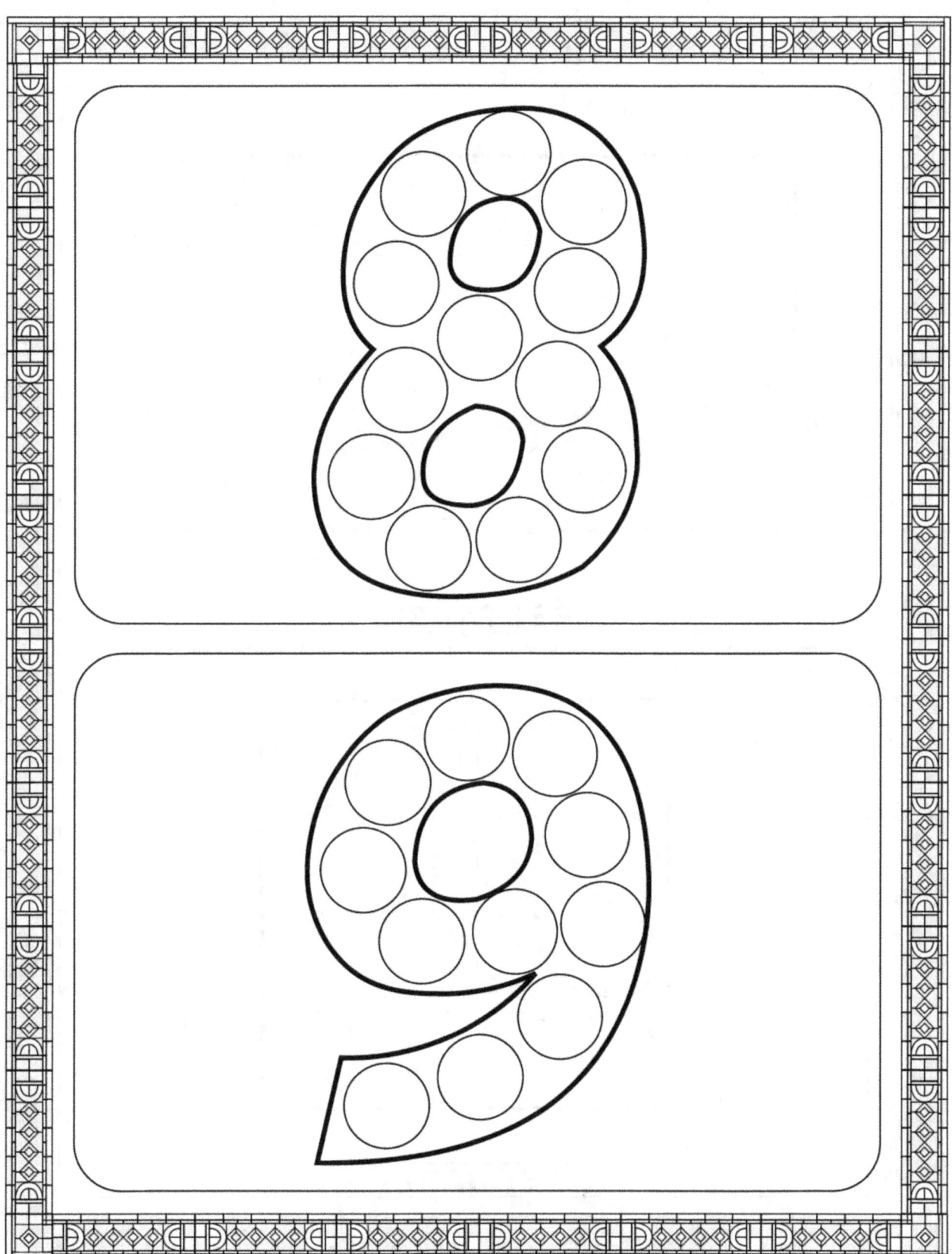

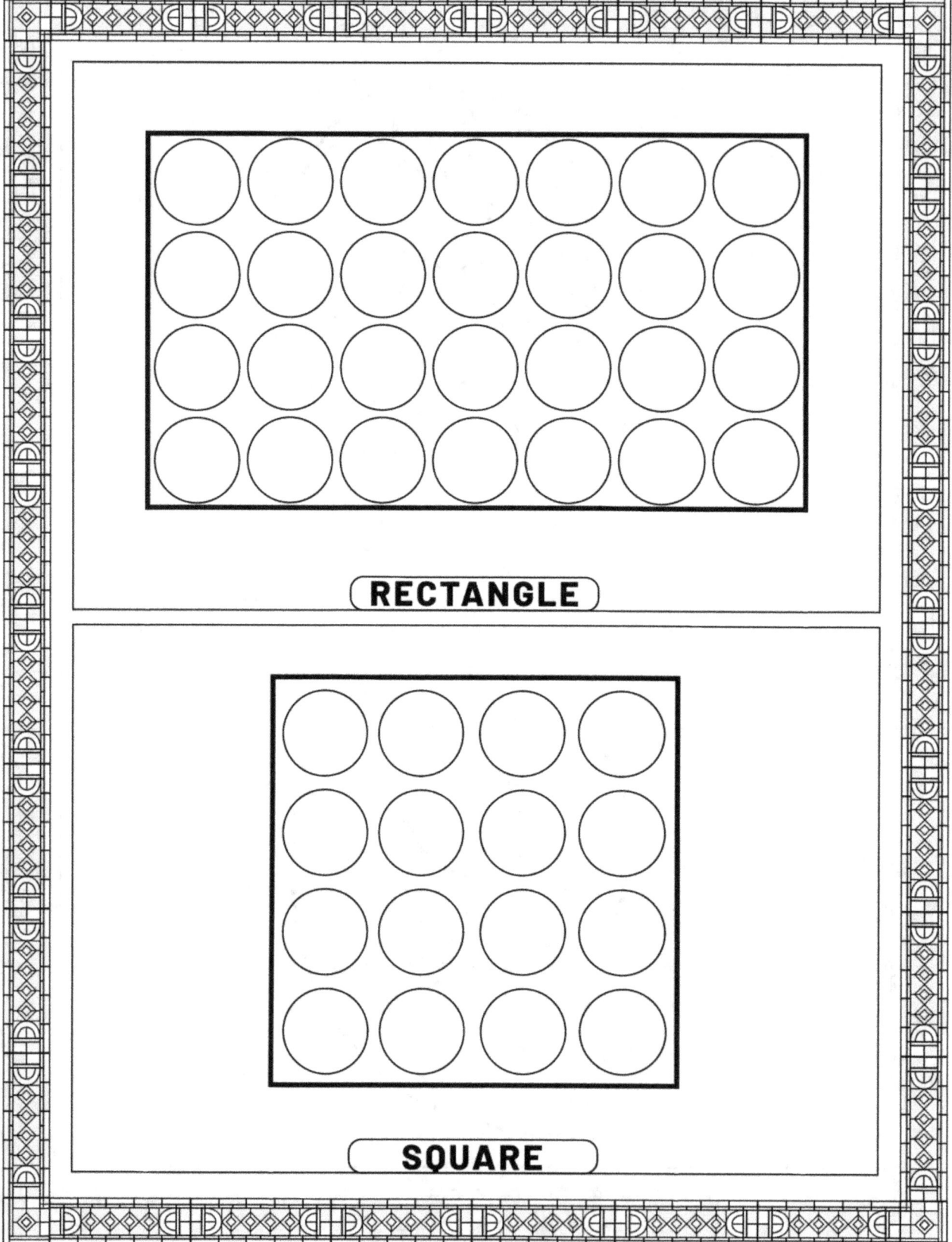

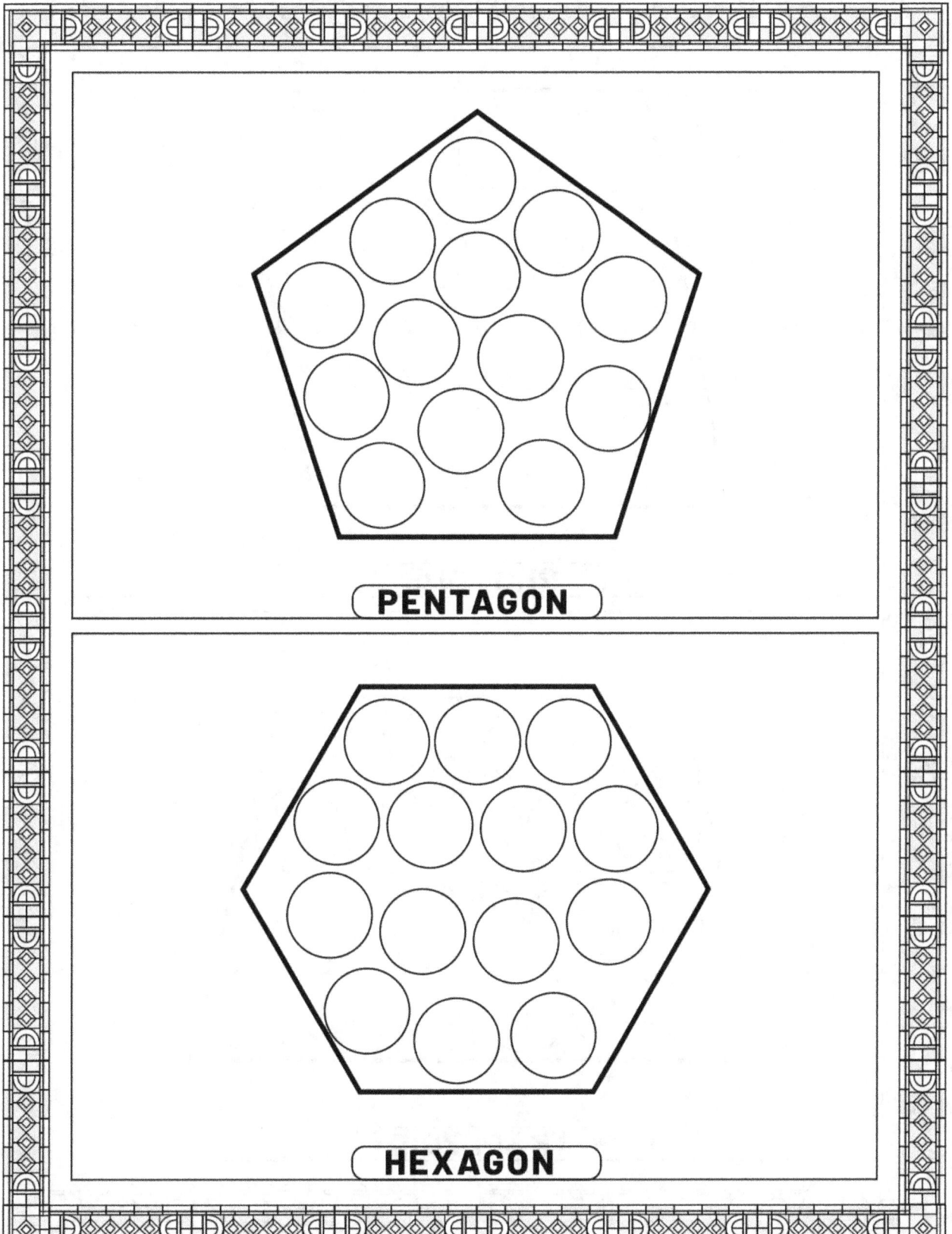

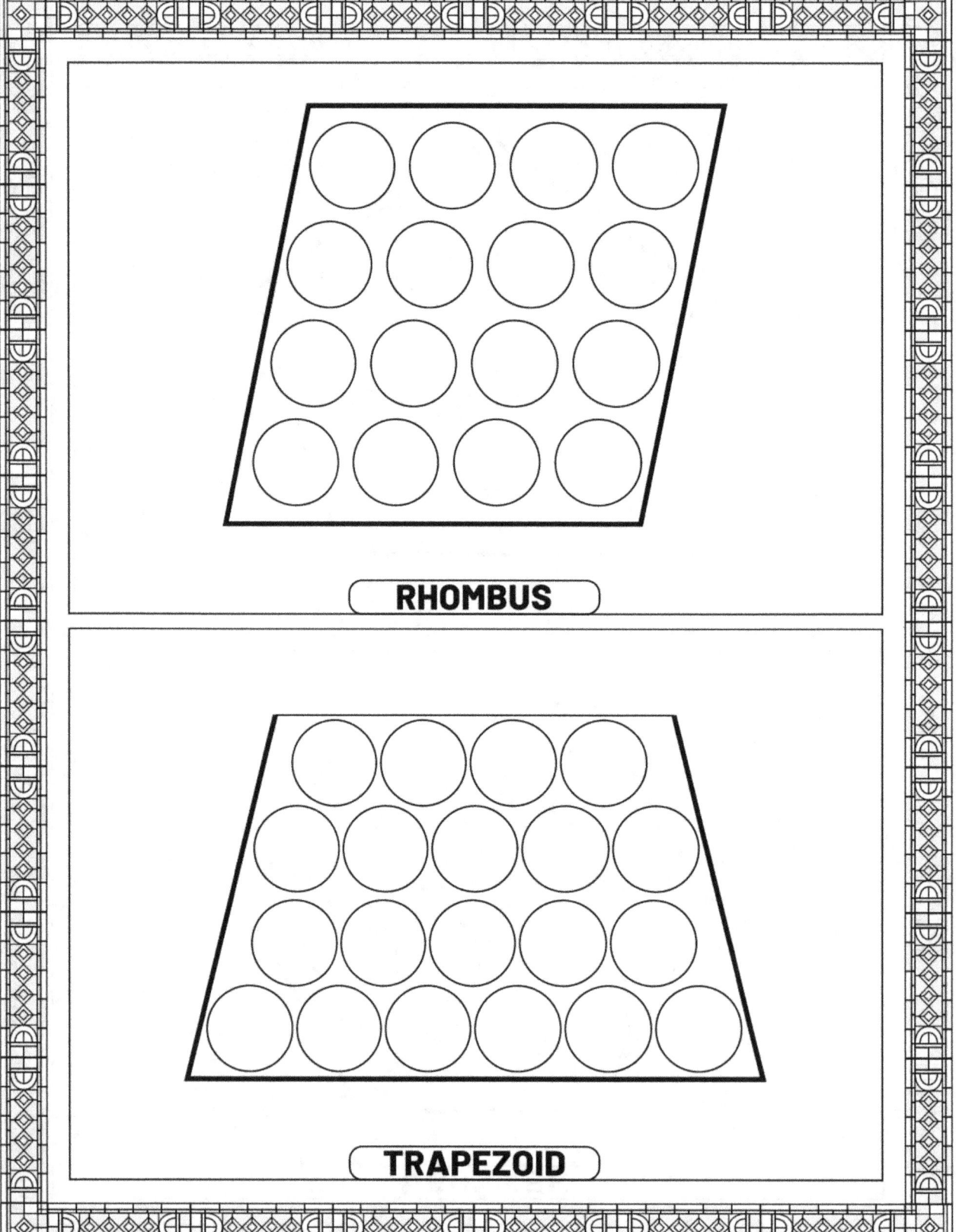

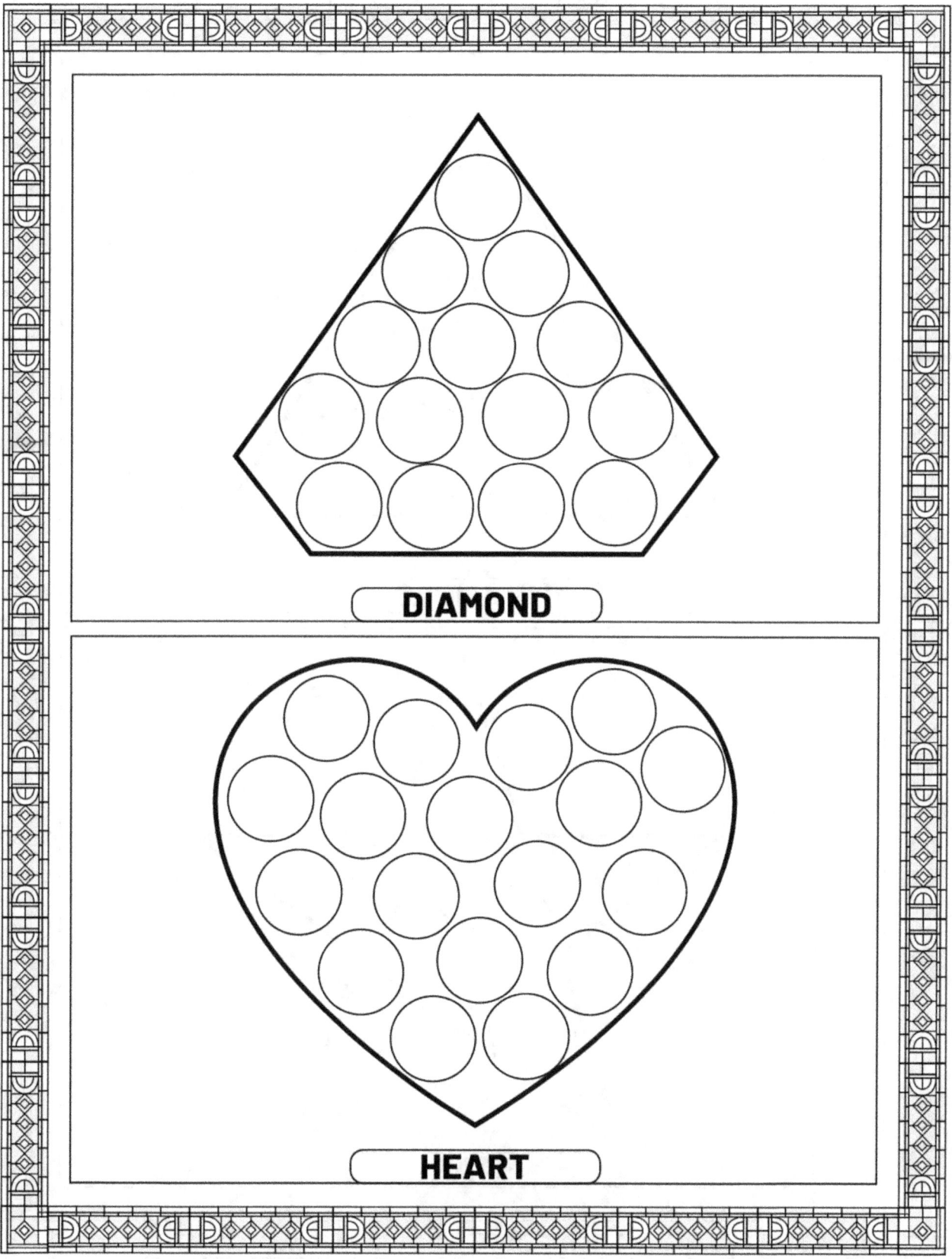

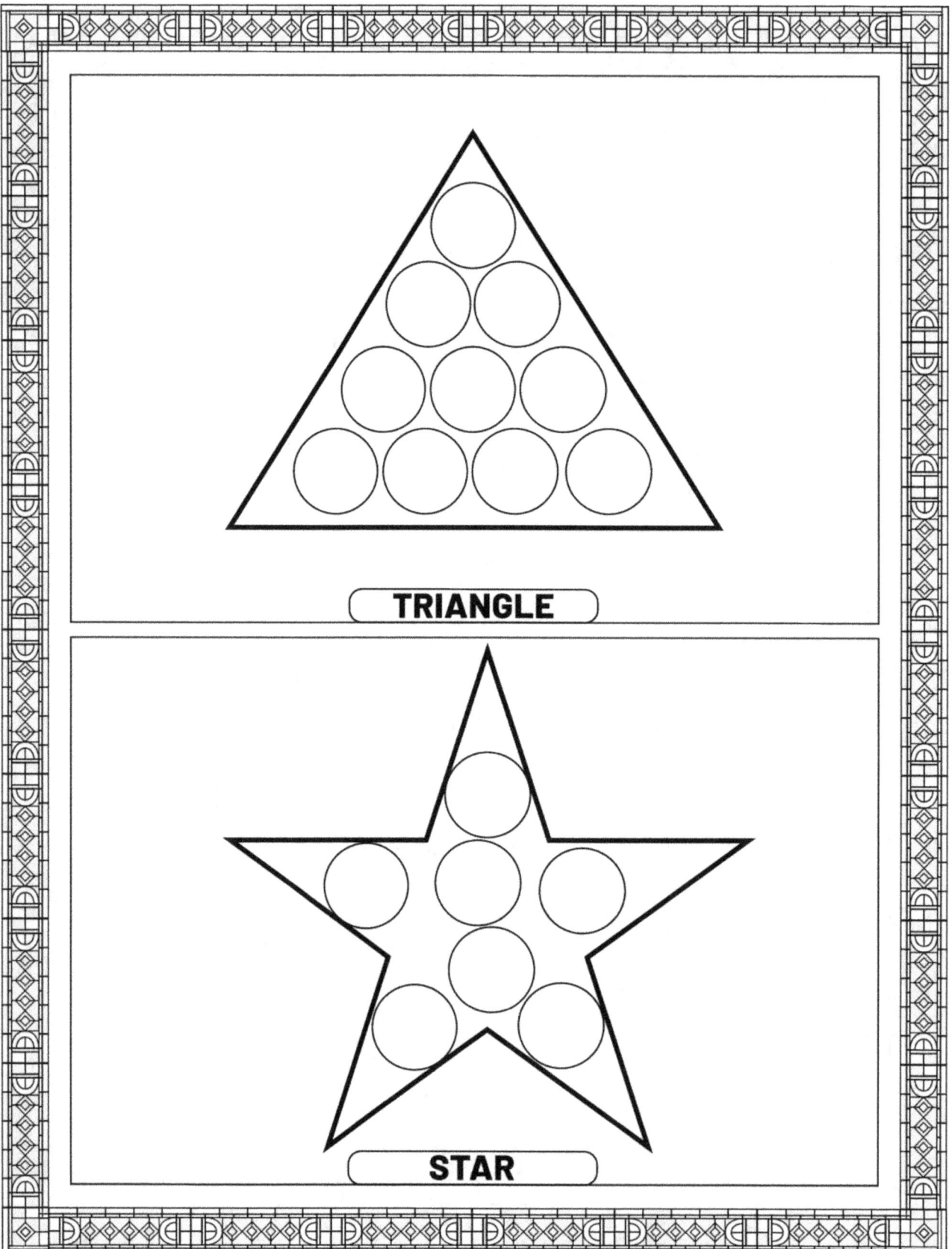

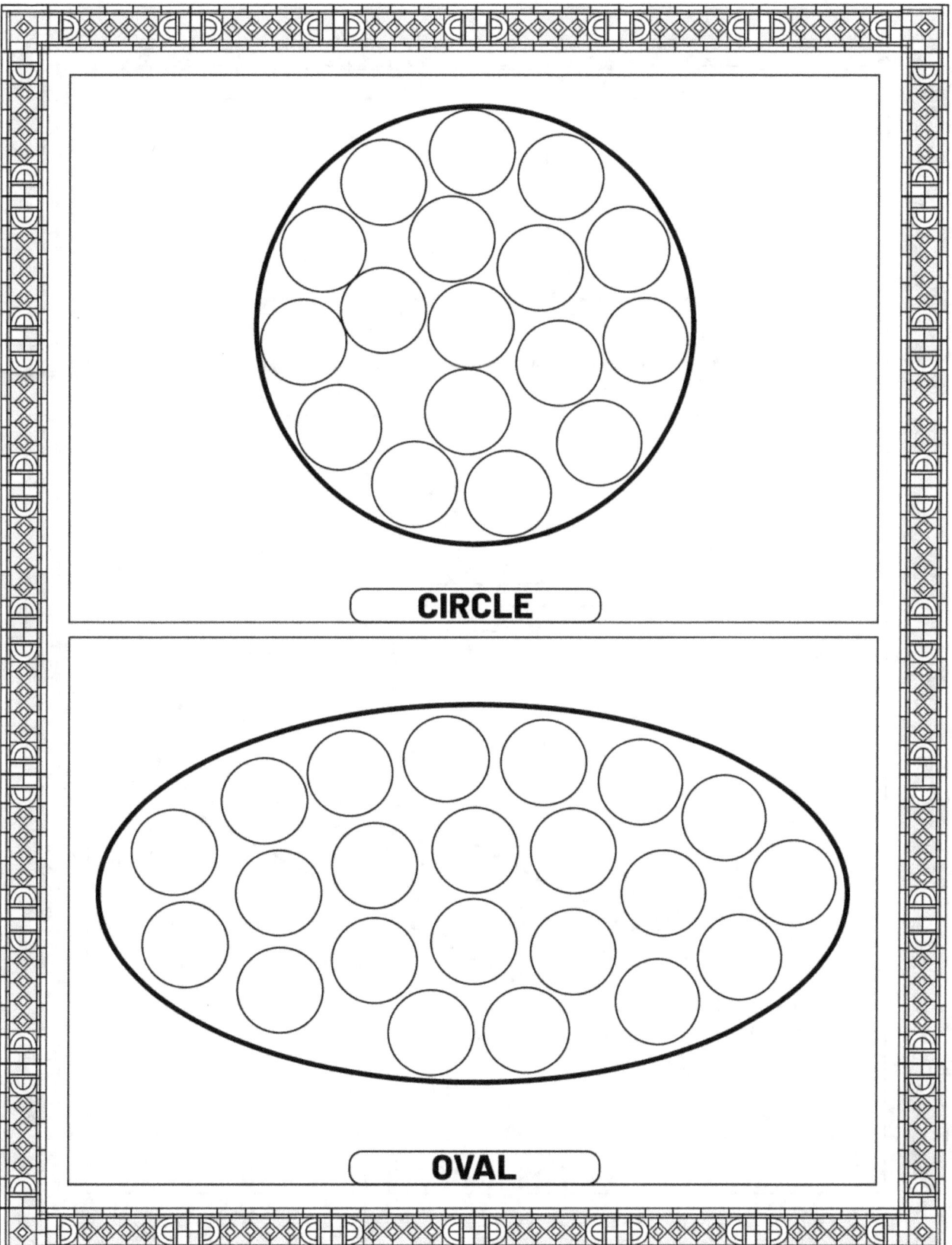

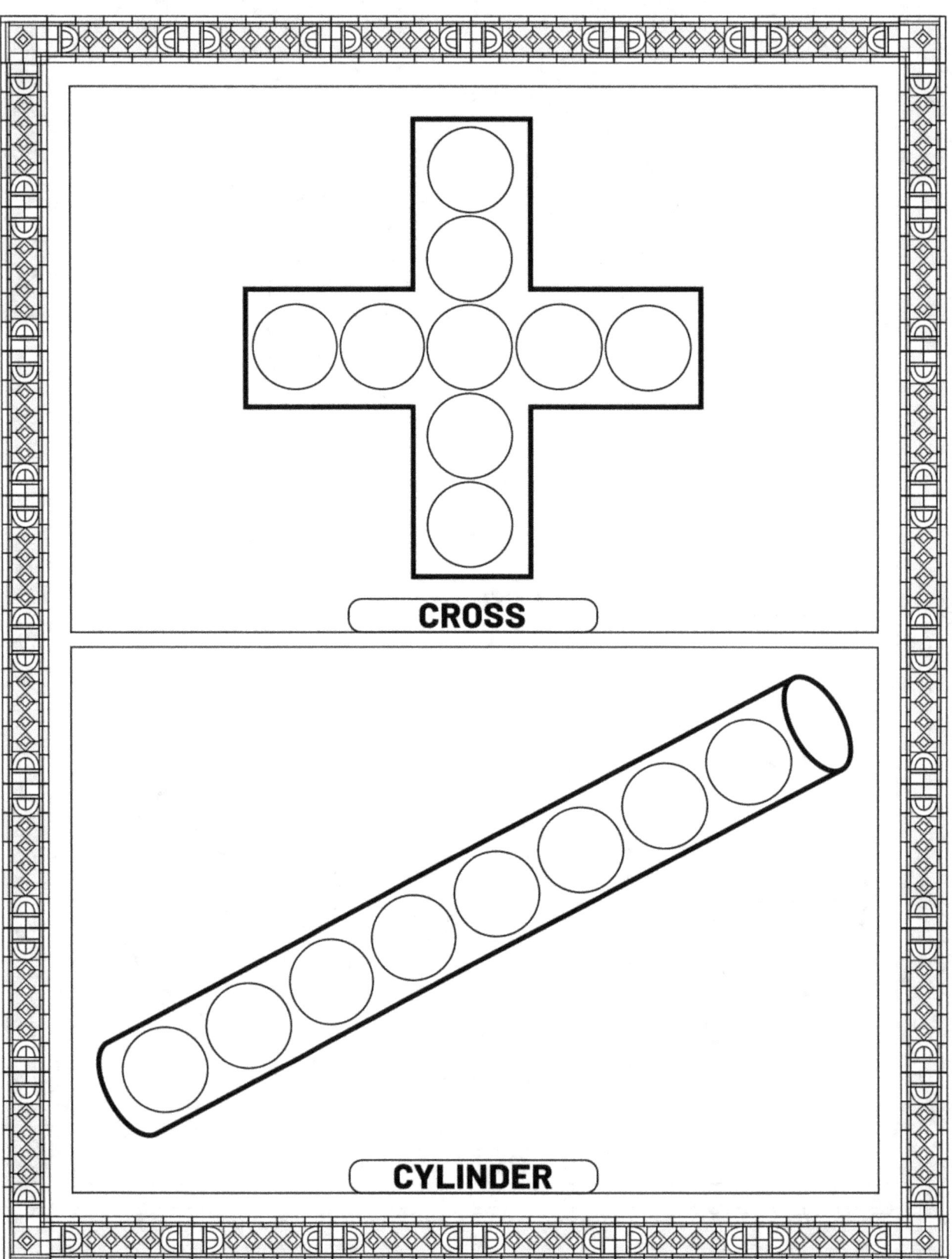

Red in nature

Number Matching

Match the digit with the word

2   one

1   five

5   seventeen

12   six

8   four

17   three

6   two

10   twelve

3   ten

4   eight

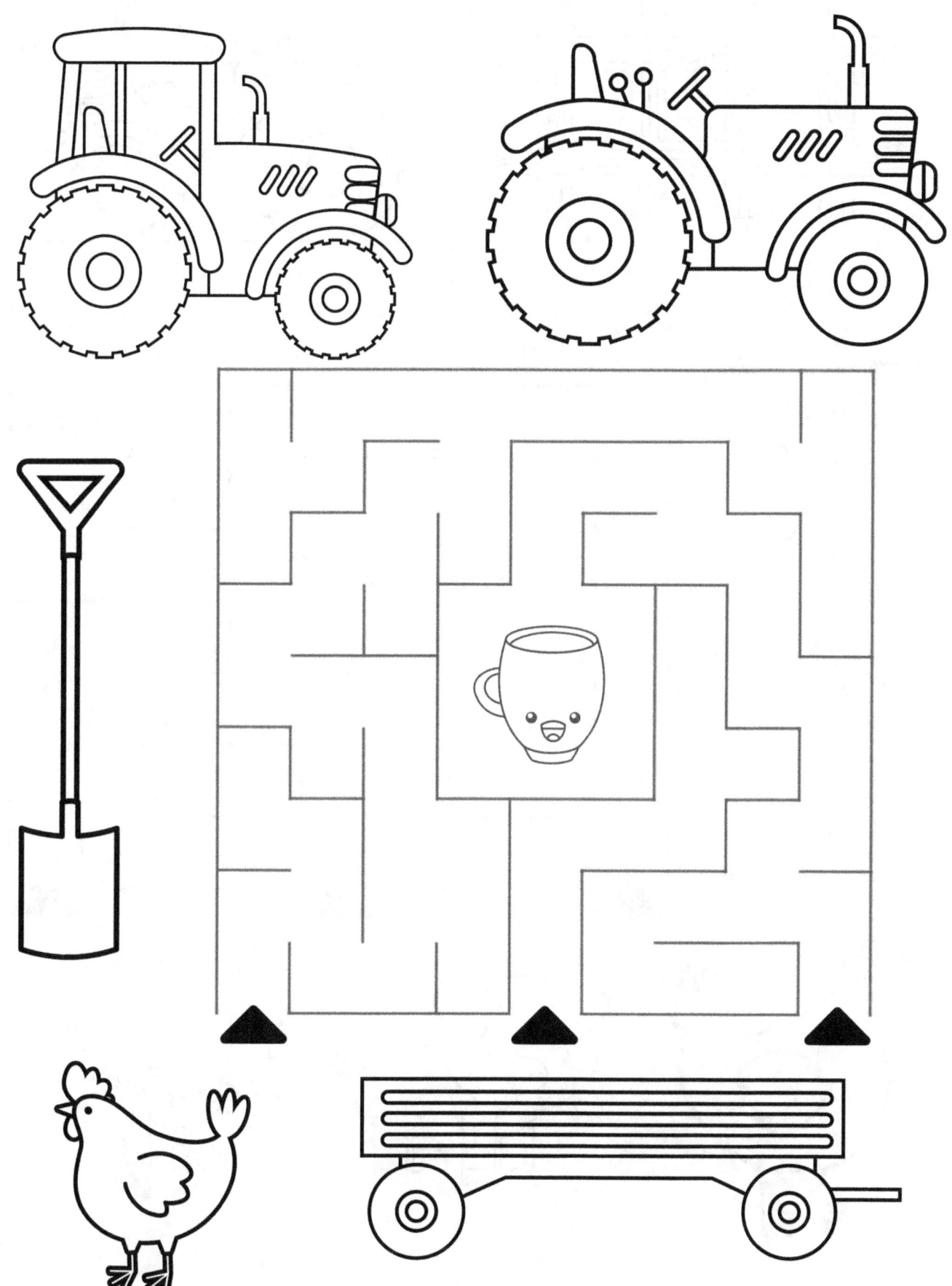

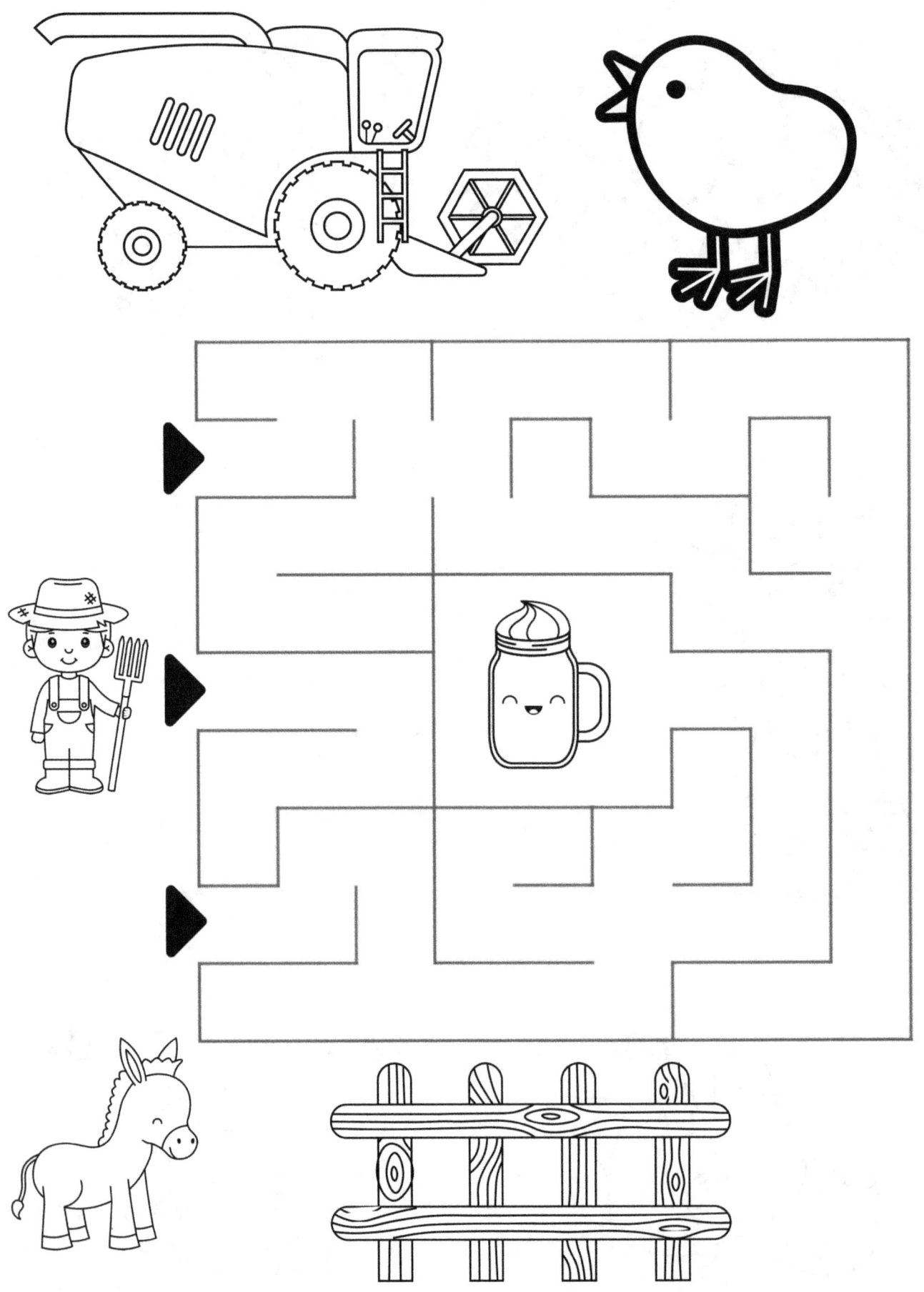

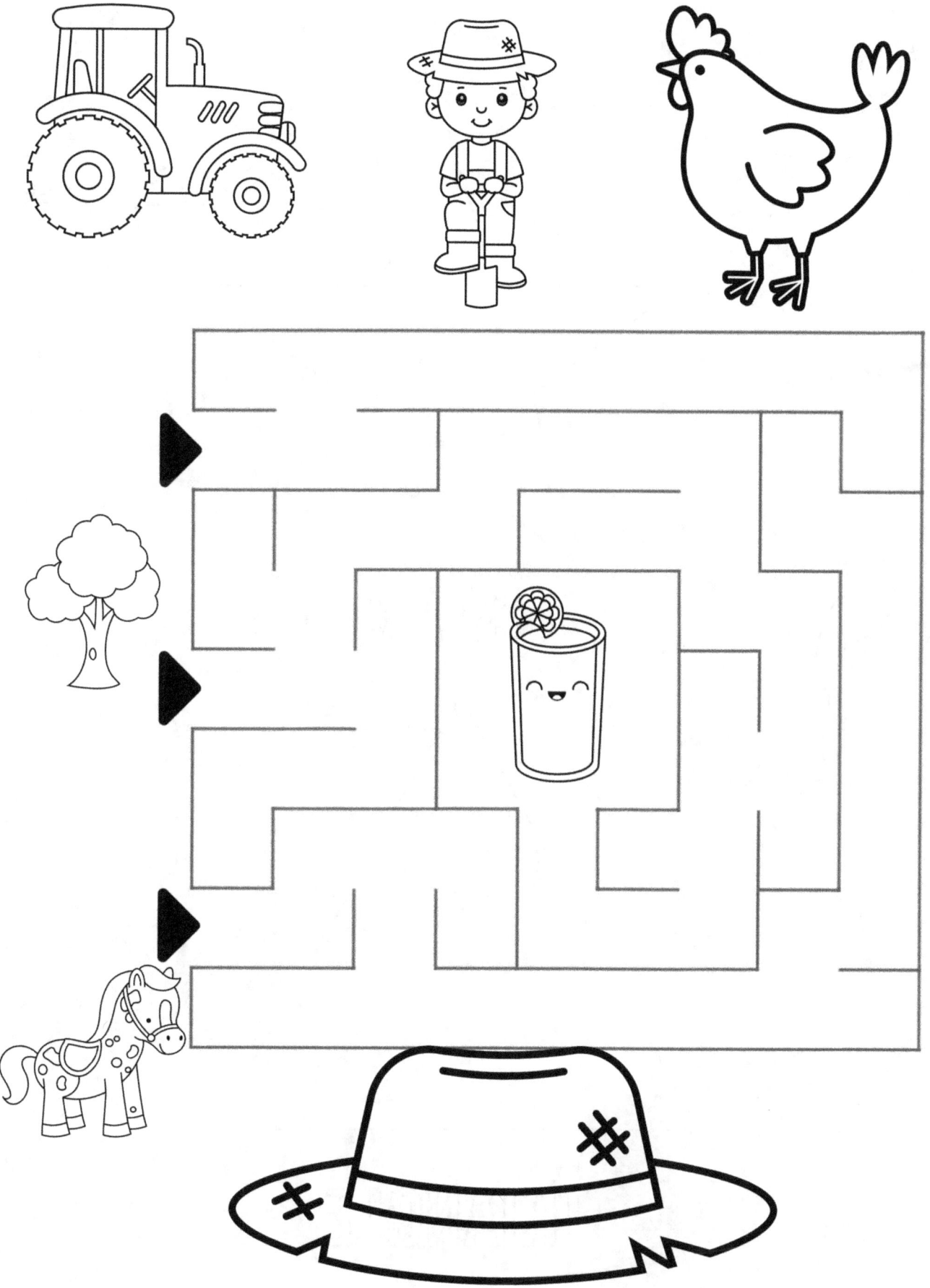

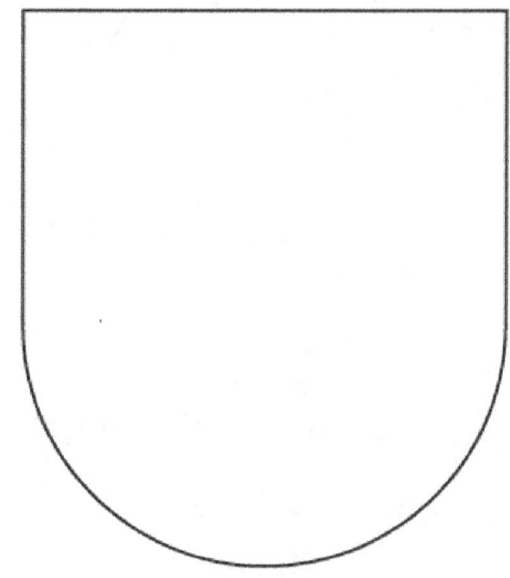

U - SHAPE

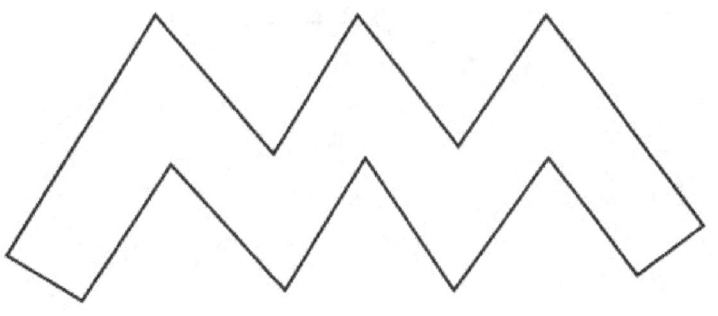

ZIG — ZAG

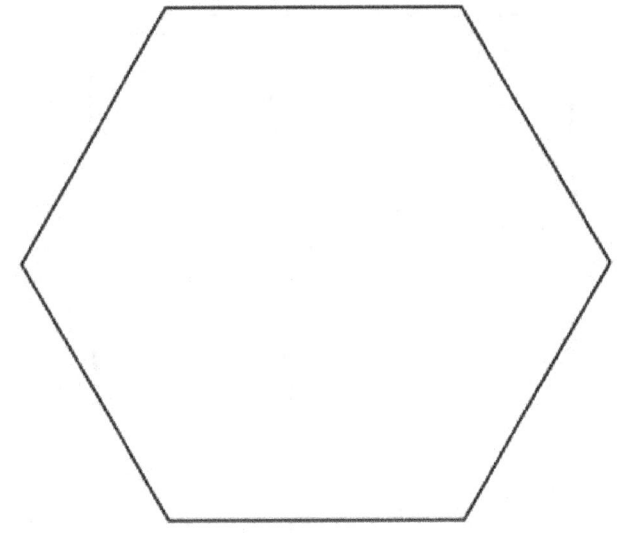

HEXAGON

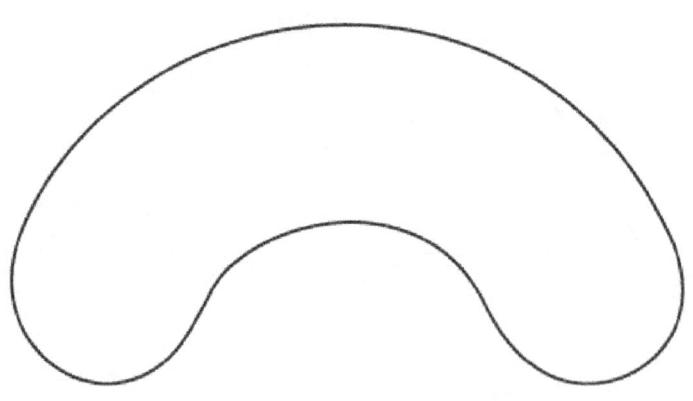

SOLID CURL